GALEN CLARK
Yosemite Guardian

.

GALEN CLARK
Yosemite Guardian

by
SHIRLEY SARGENT

FLYING SPUR PRESS • YOSEMITE, CALIFORNIA

GALEN CLARK: Yosemite Guardian
by Shirley Sargent

Copyright 1981 by Flying Spur Press

■

Some photograph credits in this book are abbreviated YNP for Yosemite National Park and SS for Shirley Sargent.

SKETCHES BY PAUL DIEDERICH

FRONTISPIECE: Galen Clark was often asked to pose in front of the Wawona Tree after the Washburn Brothers had the opening cut in 1881. (SS Collection)

Book Design by HANK JOHNSTON

Published by
FLYING SPUR PRESS
Box 278   Yosemite, CA 95389

Contents

.

This book is dedicated with appreciation to Mary Vocelka because she persuaded me that it should be revised, then helped and encouraged me throughout the months of work.

Foreword

Twenty years ago when I began the research for the original edition of this biography, my purpose was to rescue Galen Clark from undeserved obscurity. During the second half of his long life, Clark was so well known for his dedication and devotion to Yosemite as a pioneer, explorer, conservationist, author, and guardian that he was almost as famous as Half Dome. By the middle of the twentieth century, however, his valuable contributions had largely faded from public memory.

Publication of *Galen Clark, Yosemite Guardian* by the Sierra Club in 1964 focused attention on the man who served for twenty-one years as Guardian of the Yosemite Grant, and for whom Mount Clark, the Clark Range, Clark's Point, and the Clark Cottage at the Wawona Hotel were named. Unfortunately, that book has been out of print during recent years when conservation awareness has grown, and John Muir has become a folk hero. Yet Clark, who was Muir's predecessor in Yosemite by twelve years and far more intimate with its affairs, has been neglected. It was he who discovered the Mariposa Grove, kept peace with the Indians, superintended the building of trails, roads, and bridges, and zealously protected the place he described as ". . . this wonderful sanctuary of Nature's vast mountain temple."

Because old accounts not available to me previously, and new books published since 1964, gave me greater knowledge, appreciation, and insight of Clark, I determined to completely revise my text. I hope the result will redirect attention and regard to this most deserving man whom Muir called ". . . the best mountaineer I ever met."

My task was especially aided by Mary Vocelka, acting librarian of the Yosemite National Park Research Library. My access to the manuscript of a meticulous and exhaustive bibliography of Yosemite, the Big Trees, and the Sierra Nevada by Lloyd W. Currey and Ronald Kezar was another valuable asset. It directed me to rare material and library sites.

Originally, Clark descendants and Yosemite oldtimers such as Ermina L. Brayton, Leo A. McCoy, Georgia Dell McCoy, Harry Clark Regan, Will Sell, Jr., Clarence Washburn, Will Colby, and Laurence Degnan generously shared their memories and mementoes of Clark with me. Although they are all dead now, as are Carl P. Russell and Francis P. Farquhar who also helped me, their unfailing kindness and knowledge is still appreciated. Similarly, May Croop Lambert, pioneer of Summerland, was a research boon.

Mary and Bill Hood, researchers nonpareil, were of assistance on both editions of this book. Collections and staff of the Yosemite National Park Research Library, the Mariposa County Courthouse, the San Joaquin Valley Information Service, the Bancroft Library, the California State Library, and the State Archives were rewarding. In addition, I want to thank the following friends for help in research, obtaining photographs and material, and typing: Bertha Schroeder, Marilyn Fry, Jim Snyder, Dean Shenk, Jack Gyer, Wawona Washburn Hartwig, Michael Dixon, Bonney Douthit, B Weiss, Jan Clark, Betty Frost, and Karen Wood. Peg Plummer, Ann Matteson, and Hank Johnston provided sharp editorial eyes on my final draft. Finally, I thank the Sierra Club for publishing the first edition and reassigning rights to me for this second one.

Shirley Sargent
Flying Spur
April, 1981

CHAPTER I

Prelude To Paradise

.

In 1910 when Yosemite pioneer and longtime Guardian Galen Clark died, four days short of his ninety-sixth birthday, he was a distinguished and honored citizen, widely known as "Mr. Yosemite." A landmark peak and mountain range had been named for him, three books bore his byline, and after his death numerous eulogies commended him. Such position and acclaim were in sharp contrast to his reputation in the spring of 1856 when he set up a shelter alongside the verdant meadow at Wawona on the South Fork of the Merced River. Then forty-two, an abject failure in business and family life, he was a condemned man; as he said, "given up to die at any hour" of consumption.

One of the fourteen children of Mary and Jonas Clark, Galen had been born near Shipton, Quebec, on March 28, 1814. His father was more interested in collecting and selling medicinal herbs than farming, hence the name Galen, commemorating a famed Greek physician. Four of the children died in Canada, partly due to malnutrition. By 1819, the Clarks were forced to return to their former home, Dublin, New Hampshire, where 1,260 residents lived near Mount Monadnock.

"Galen was placed in the home of a friend from the age of five to seventeen years," an historian explained, "because the family was so large." He saw his parents frequently, however, attended school and church with his brothers and sisters, and revered his family. He was a sickly, quiet boy, loving, devout, and perceptive. Reverend Levi Leonard, pastor of the town's Unitarian church, superintendent of its schools, and founder of its library, the first free public library in America, had a strong, beneficial influence on Galen and his brothers.

At seventeen, Galen was sent to Genesee, New York, to learn chair-making and housepainting from a cousin. Before he reached twenty-one, he had applied those trades in Boston and Philadelphia. By then he was a broad-shouldered, handsome man about 5′9″ with thick, brown hair, and penetrating blue eyes under a wide, unlined brow. Integrity radiated from him and he impressed people with his courtesy and gentleness. In fact, he tried to live by the precepts of the Holy Bible and *The American Chesterfield*, a guide to manners and morals, which he owned and studied. His formal education had been limited to grammar school and one term at an academy, but he widened his knowledge by reading many periodicals and books. Although never robust, he was restless and adventurous enough to try his luck in the unsettled West. At twenty-three, he explored Iowa and Illinois before settling in northeastern Missouri, where the land, streams, and timber promised, he wrote his brother William, "flattering prospects." His purchase of 160 acres with money borrowed from William proved disastrous as crop failure, "a great drowth," "a violent cold," and an injured leg befell him.

After that he became a furniture maker but made more coffins than chairs, and pay was slow to non-

9

Character and integrity radiated from young Galen Clark in this Philadelphia photograph, circa 1853. (YNP Collection)

George Faber Clark, one of Galen's five brothers, became a Unitarian minister and foster father to Clark's son Alonzo. (YNP Collection)

existent. His debts, ill health, and the possibility of death haunted him. His one piece of good fortune was his friendship with the Joseph McCoy family, in whose home he stayed most of the time and whose eighteen-year-old daugther, Rebecca, he wed in 1839. Despite McCoy's moral and financial help, the marriage was plagued with misfortunes almost from the start. Because of "sickness which I shall never get well of," Galen could not tend his farm, could not finish paying for it, and used his last borrowed $200 for a grocery business that also failed. His wife's illness and the birth of children, law suits, and unpaid time away in the so-called Mormon War further impoverished him. His distress, mirrored in letters home, was agonizing. Three of his brothers were established and doing well, but Galen, like his father, was improvident. "Dear Brother," Galen addressed William, who wanted his loan repaid, "I am in trouble and know not what to do . . . I assure you I will pay you as soon as I can."

What he did was return to Philadelphia to work for his former employer, painting houses at $30 a month. There, nine days after their fifth child was born in Feb-

ruary, 1848, Rebecca Clark died of consumption. Galen's debts increased, his health worsened, and he could not care properly for his children. Within two years, he left them with his parents and an unmarried sister and set off for Texas in search of health and income. Both eluded him there and, next, in New York, where he worked as a painter.

While in that city he visited its Crystal Palace and was entranced by an exhibit that displayed information on California's climate and quantities of gold. By 1853 California's allure had magnetized thousands of Easterners, first to the gold fields and, later, to the fields of agriculture and commerce. Galen could not resist the hope of health and wealth and boarded ship in October, 1853, for San Francisco, where he arrived on November 21. His introduction to that city was inauspicious, for prices were exorbitant and winter fogs unhealthful. He soon left for the Gold Country.

Galen's first prospecting efforts were in Mariposa County at the southern end of the rich Mother Lode. "Mining," he said later, "was the hardest kind of work, digging, shoveling, lifting, and working in the water, most of the time in raw, winter weather." Despite such labor, he found barely enough gold for subsistence. "As I never met with any success with mining for myself," he said, "I worked with a mining company as assistant, as packer and camp-keeper of the Mariposa Ditch Company. That was in 1855."

Surveying for the Company took him into trail-less wilderness along the South Fork of the Merced River where beauty and game were abundant. R. H. Ogg, the camp hunter, regaled the crew with tales of three monstrous trees he had encountered deep in the mountains; they also heard of an amazing valley with waterfalls two-thousand feet high and cliffs that shut out the sun. It had been explored by members of the Mariposa Battalion in 1851, when they had entered it in pursuit of Indians. Such tales sounded incredible even after they were described in a July, 1855, *Mariposa Gazette* by an Englishman named James Mason Hutchings. He wrote of five days spent in "luxurious scenic banqueting" in the seven-mile-long, mile-wide chasm. Furthermore, an artist in his party had documented the height of the cliffs and waterfalls with sketches. A waterfall over two-thousand feet high? Surely not, Clark thought, and yet even the canyon walls along the South Fork were almost double the height of Mount Monadnock, the giant of his childhood. What a thrill it would be to view the natural wonders in the incredible valley!

Like-minded miners talked it over, and in August, seventeen of them, including Galen, organized a horseback party and rode off on a dim Indian track. His reaction to Yosemite Valley, written and published decades later, described the awe he felt on the excursion:

> We spent several days . . . wandering and exploring and viewing the grandeur and sublimity . . . worshipping in this wonderful sanctuary, this sanctum sanctorum of Nature's vast mountain temple . . .

He mentioned "the great abundance of wildflowers and luxuriant grass reaching to our saddle skirts." Sugarpines, fir, cedar, and ponderosa pines "of such beauty, grace and symmetry of form were a new and wonderful revelation to me." He saw that Yosemite Falls, though at a summer low in volume, did indeed descend over 2,000 feet, and Half Dome neared 9,000 feet in elevation.

Another group of miners camped in the Valley at the same time, and in October, a fourth tourist party composed of Mariposans and San Franciscans explored it. That year 43 white men, inspired by James Hutchings' rhapsodic descriptions, visited Yosemite Valley. Six of those sightseers were so impressed with the singular

Clark became enchanted by the beauties of Yosemite, including Yosemite Falls. (George Fiske, YNP Collection)

"We spent several days . . . worshipping in this wonderful sanctuary . . ." Clark wrote of his August, 1855, visit to Yosemite Valley. (Thomas Hill painting, Original in Oakland Museum)

magnificence that their lives were ever afterward involved with its promotion and development. Three of them were journalists: Hutchings, who began editing his *California Magazine* the following year; James H. Lawrence, writer and later editor of a Mariposa newspaper; and L.A. Holmes, editor of the year-old *Mariposa Gazette*. Miners Milton and Houston Mann, who ran a livery stable in Mariposa, combined with their brother Andrew to build a horse trail from Mariposa to the Valley. Galen Clark was the sixth.

After that epic trip, he returned to more exhausting, unrewarding mining and, Lawrence stated, "a brief ex-perience with a mountain sawmill." On March 19, 1856, Clark filed a land claim "for agricultural and growing purposes" of 160 acres at the meadow near the South Fork of the Merced. The expansive, forest-encircled meadow had made a logical campsite for the miners in 1855, as it was roughly twenty-five miles from Mariposa and about the same distance from Yosemite Valley. Timber, game, water, and horse feed were profuse. About the time of filing the land claim, Galen suffered what he called "a severe attack of hemorrhage of the lungs from which I was given up to die at any hour." Death, which he had long feared, seemed imminent.

CHAPTER II

A Good Place To Stay

■

Despite the dire prophecy, Clark's ingrained optimism kept him from complete despair, and his land claim suggested a refuge. Its wealth of sun, invigorating mountain air, and quietude promised serenity — possibly even healing. "I went to the mountains," he was to recall, "to take my chances of dying or growing better which I thought were about even." His campsite was in a glade on the northwestern fringe of the large natural meadow. The South Fork was less than a thousand feet away, but he developed a spring within a few yards of his camp. Pine trees encircled him on three sides, while the fourth was open to the meadow and the mountains to the east. For a doomed man, who, he stated, "spent the first season in leisure," he was remarkably active, ". . . fishing, hunting grouse, deer, and occasionally grizzly bears, and roughing it generally — going bareheaded and sometimes barefooted . . ." His theory was that poor circulation caused headaches and cold feet, so he disdained "boots and shoes as cruel and silly instruments of torture, at once uncivilized, inhuman and unnecessary." Another health theory he practiced was roasting and eating deer liver. As deer had no gall, their liver, he thought, would help cure consumption.

Although three other men had filed land claims in the area, Clark's nearest white neighbor was sixteen miles away; he was not completely alone, however, for a small band of Indians befriended him. They gave him fish and game, aided him with heavy tasks, sometimes camped near him, and taught him their ways and history. Clark observed their skills and their natural conservation of land and animals and learned to respect them.

In keeping with his hand-to-mouth existence, Galen's appearance was rough and unkempt, gaunt and bearded. His active life in "the pure, cold, soft mountain air, and the exhilarating atmosphere of these grand forests" slowly restored his health and recharged his energy. Where he spent that winter is not known, but in April, 1857, he built a log cabin on the opposite side of the meadow. This sloping site was freer from dampness and mosquitoes, and had a more commanding view. His windowless cabin was 12 feet by 16 feet, but usually the plank door stood hospitably open. Blazing fires in a rock fireplace added light and warmth. A contemporary claimed that an Indian woman shared his primitive home. No documentation exists, but he was in need of care, lonely and ill.

Indoors he utilized his old trade and made a bed, three-legged stools, cupboards, and shelves. Large sugar pinecones, antlers, and deer and bear skins decorated the walls, and books such as a Bible, *Pilgrim's Progress*, and Thackerey's *The Newcomes* graced his shelves. Before long, the Indians called his home Pallahchun, meaning "A good place to stop."

Clark's most frequent white visitors were Milton, Houston, and Andrew Mann. These energetic brothers were improving their horse trail to Yosemite Valley,

"I went to the mountains," Clark said, "to take my chances of dying or growing better... fishing, hunting, going bareheaded and sometimes barefooted." (Carleton Watkins, YNP Collection)

Clark's first cabin was sketched from his description by artist Thomas Hill for the June 2, 1895, **San Francisco Chronicle.**

which had opened in August, 1856. Tolls of $2.00 each way for anyone on horseback, $2.00 for each pack mule, and $1.00 per footman were set by the Mariposa Board of Supervisors and recorded in the Supervisors' Minutes, now preserved in the venerable Mariposa Courthouse along with other invaluable documentation.

At first, traffic and tolls were meager and mainly derived from ex-miners who were ready to exchange gold pans for axes, saws, and hammers with which they built rude ferries, lodgings, and barns in Yosemite Valley in anticipation of tourist trade. Hutchings' descriptions, accompanied by lithographs, published in his new 1856 *California Magazine*, had already begun to attract travel. Other discouraged miners turned to farming or developing sawmills, stables, and hotels in and around Mariposa. To the north, Lafayette Bunnell and George Coulter had built a trail between Coulterville and Yosemite Valley, which immediately established competition and rivalry between Mariposa and Coulterville businessmen.

As the Mann, or Mariposa Trail passed his place, Clark was a witness and participant in its usage. In 1857 he helped the brothers build the first bridge across the South Fork and encountered camping parties who stopped nearby en route to the Valley. "On their return trip," he wrote later, "they would be out of provisions, and as I always had a good supply of fresh venison and trout, they would call upon me for meals." Satisfied travelers, unaware of the Indian title Pallahchun, referred to his place as Clark's Station.

Clark cooked over an outdoor firepit where he roasted venison, grouse, trout, squirrels, and potatoes for appreciative guests such as the five women who arrived at 9:30 p.m. on a May night in 1857. One of them, Harriet Kirtland, kept a journal in which she recorded,

> Mr. Clark cooked us some venison . . . and I never tasted anything half so good and the bread too. He let us have the bunk to sleep in, it seemed so strange the house is made of large logs, ground for the floor and a monstrous large place for the fire. He was very kind. Showed us every attention, said he had never had ladies visit him before.

Much of his time was spent hunting and exploring, gaining an intimate knowledge of the Yosemite region, its geology, geography, and botany. His special love was trees, and he said that he liked "nothing in the world better than climbing to the top of a high ridge or mountain and looking off." He came home with more mountaineering experience and a pack full of meat to share with wayfarers.

On such excursions, he kept a sharp eye out for the three monstrous trees the hunter Ogg had reported. Finally, in late May, 1857, while he and Milton Mann were hunting game southeast of and above the meadow, they came upon a whole grove of red-barked Sequoias. In awe they gazed upward to the tops some two hundred feet above them. Here were living, growing trees that had survived thousands of years. In wonder and excitement, Galen measured the massive girth of one and estimated a circumference of forty-five feet. Yet the giant's cones were no bigger than a hen's egg, solid and sculptured but tiny.

Afterwards Mann could scarcely wait to begin a trail to the grove, which gave the Mariposa route a scenic advantage over the Coulterville Trail north of Yosemite Valley. Two small groves of Sequoias grew on the northside, but the trail bypassed them. When stage roads were built in 1874, that was rectified. The Coulterville Road arrowed through the Merced Grove, and the Big Oak Flat Road wound around the Tuolumne Grove. In the interim, however, the Mariposa route capitalized on the Mariposa Grove as a tourist attraction.

Within weeks, Clark thoroughly explored the area, locating two distinct groves and counting the trees in each. The Upper Grove contained 265 mature Sequoias, the lower 241. "Several months later," he was to recall, "I found the three trees described by Mr. Ogg in a gulch some distance from their fellows." As all the giants were in Mariposa County "I named them the Mariposa Grove of Big Trees." Later admirers suggested that the grove be renamed in his honor, but he steadfastly refused the proposal.

Well-wishers did rename the first tree he had seen, and dubbed Forest Queen, the Galen Clark tree, but he removed the sign. As time passed, guides and tourists named many of the outstanding Sequoias, and their historic, patriotic, and fanciful titles adorned signs that were nailed onto the thick cinnamon-colored bark. By 1863, Hutchings recorded such titles as King Arthur, Washington, Lafayette, Mrs. J.C. Fremont, Grizzly Giant, and Satan's Spear. That Clark himself joined, at least briefly, in the naming mania was evident in the sign Monadnock and his Forest Queen.

His Indian friends told him their name for the big trees was Wah-no-nah, and that another large grove existed several miles southeast. Clark enlisted an Indian to guide him to the grove in the fall of 1857. Again he was astonished by the throngs of trees which he estimated as more than five hundred in number; again he explored, publicized, and named the grove after its home county. The name Fresno Grove of Big Trees was retained even after a boundary change placed it in Madera County, but, still later, it was renamed Nelder Grove after a hermit who lived amid its solitude. Many of the trees were cut down by loggers in the early 1880's — a devastating waste because a large amount of the wood splintered in the felling.

Clark loved wandering in the woods, but circumstances forced him into a more stay-at-home role, as regular tourist travel to the Mariposa Grove and Yosemite Valley commenced in 1857. "I began to give entertainment at my place," he said, "and as travel increased I increased my accommodations." In May he had told Harriet Kirtland, quoted earlier, that he intended "to

Clark discovered the legions of giant sequoia trees southeast of Wawona and named them the Mariposa Grove of Big Trees. (Putnam and Valentine, SS Collection)

erect a house to accommodate visitors." Admittedly comforts were scarce, yet travelers were rugged rather than fastidious, weary, and grateful to have shelter and food. Clark's charges were moderate and inconsistent, for his experiences had made him a pushover for a hardluck story. What little cash he accumulated was invested in supplies rather than going along with his own hardluck letters to his brothers.

It is unlikely that he billed photographers or artists for board since their efforts in picturing the region promoted publicity and more travel. Charles L. Weed was the first photographer to visit, and Clark was so fascinated by the man and his cumbersome equipment of a forty-pound camera, heavy glass plates, chemicals, non-folding tripod, and a tent to use as a darkroom that he guided Weed to choice spots in the Mariposa Grove and helped him load and unload pack mules. Two years later, in 1861, Carleton E. Watkins, another pioneer lensman, arrived with twelve mules laden with photographic essentials. Clark guided him to the Big Trees, then posed at the base of the Grizzly Giant for a classic frontiersman picture. In return for his kindness, Weed, Watkins, and other photographers gave Clark fine views of Yosemite Valley and the Sequoia trees he revered.

During that same year, landscape artist Albert Bierstadt was welcomed and guided by Clark, who again posed at the base of the Grizzly Giant, this time for inclusion in an enormous painting, which was sold to a collector.

Galen had to go to Mariposa for mail, so it was months after his son's death in December, 1857, before he had the news. Nine-year-old Solon McCoy Clark had fallen through ice and drowned in a pond. Five years later, son Joseph, nineteen, was killed in a Civil War battle. Although an absentee father, Clark had kept in touch with his children and must have grieved. In 1864, Galen Alonzo Clark, his sole surviving son, enlisted in the Union Army. Because of his sons' involvement, Clark followed what war news reached him with particular interest. He was a Union supporter, who placed photographs of President Lincoln and Generals Sherman and Sheridan in his photograph album. Clark later met Sherman, Sheridan, and U.S. Grant, on their respective post-war visits to Yosemite.

Hutchings estimated that seven-hundred tourists visited Yosemite between 1855 and 1864, less than one hundred a year, of which at least half traveled by the Mann Trail and stopped at Clark's Station. These pioneer travelers were hardy, questing souls, well aware that they were in the vanguard of sightseers, awed, but hardly silenced by the wonders they witnessed. Inspiration Point, well above the present-day Wawona Tunnel, constituted the springboard for response. "Here all who make California books," said geologist Clarence King, who himself wrote one of them, "down to the last and most sentimental specimen who so much as meditates a letter to his or her local newspaper, dismounts and inflates."

While indulging in rhetoric, many pen-pushing travelers described Yosemite's accommodations and the pioneers who provided them. Clark's character and the evolution of his stopping place received generous mention: perhaps the best of it was printed in travel accounts. One, published in a Boston newspaper, told of a July day when eight tired men had dismounted at Clark's. The writer described it as "a little log house and canvas tent on a meadow in the wilderness . . . Mr. Clarke we found a very intelligent man, living alone in the wilderness. To my amazement he knew me. He was born under the shadow of Monadnock, and had two brothers, I soon learned, who are Unitarian ministers." The chronicler was none other than Thomas Starr King, a noted Unitarian minister himself, who had recently left his native New England to become pastor of the First Unitarian Church in San Francisco. King enjoyed Clark's hot biscuits at supper, but not the snarling of his "large wolf-dog" who woke him "beneath our roof of cotton cloth . . . At four we were up from our couches, and before six were mounted for the Yosemite."

By 1862 a traveler reported that two small tents and Clark's log cabin made up a practical but ramshackle lodging place. An 1863 visitor raved about the speckled trout and wild strawberries Galen provided, but fretted about his charges of "4 bits a meal. I don't see how he lives, for a dollar a meal would be little enough . . . but perhaps he has other customers as generous as we were. We [five] took three meals a day and gave him $15.00 . . ." Two years later a diary-keeping woman noted that Clark's

> . . . house was a slight frame building of three rooms with a piazza before and behind dust all around it. Other buildings for the kitchen and accommodation of the ordinary backwoodsman were clustered about the midst of an inclosure, in which and beyond as far as eye could see were stately trees — but no grass anywhere.

Fritz Ludlow, who had accompanied Bierstadt in 1863, later described his Yosemite experience in a magazine and book that were complimentary to Clark. His brothers must have been amazed and proud to see their ne'er-do-well sibling praised first in the *Boston Evening Transcript* by Thomas Starr King, and then in Ludlow's 1864 *Atlantic Monthly* article:

> Clark himself is one of the best informed men, one of the very best guides, I ever met in the California or any other wilderness. He is a fine-looking, stalwart old grizzly hunter and miner of the '49 days, wears a noble full beard

Clark built this cabin in the spring of 1864 so visitors to the Mariposa Grove would have shelter. Today, a museum stands on the site. (YNP Collection)

hued like his favorite game, but no head-covering of any kind since recovered from a fever which left his head intolerant of even a slouch. He lives among folk, near Mariposa, in winter, and in summer occupies a hermitage built by himself in one of the loveliest, lofty valleys of the Sierra. Here he gives travelers a surprise by the nicest poached eggs and rashers of bacon, home-made bread and wild-strawberry sweetmeats which they will find in the State.

Obviously Clark's culinary skills over a campfire were more advanced than his practices as a businessman, yet he was learning that an innkeeper in an undeveloped area had to be a man of parts. Farming had never been his intent, but to satisfy guests' needs, he kept chickens, hogs, cattle, and eventually a small dairy herd. He planted apple trees, potatoes, vegetables, and hay. He paid Indians to care for his crops. After the Civil War, land on the other side of the South Fork was homesteaded, which gave Clark a source of produce and labor.

Besides being a rancher and host, he was a hunter, cook, entertainer, and guide as well as promoter, publicist, surveyor, and even common laborer. After Mariposa County purchased the Mann brothers' trail for $200 in 1860, Clark was appointed Road Overseer, a dubious position without honor or pay. Often he himself had to wield shovel, axe, and pry-bar. Tumultuous storms in January, 1862, severely damaged trail and crossings, and Mariposans subscribed $300 toward re-

Preservation was almost unknown when the Yosemite Grant, protecting Yosemite Valley and the Mariposa Grove, was created in June, 1864. The land was granted to the state of California "to be held for public use, resort, and recreation . . . inalienable for all time. (Hank Johnston Collection)

pair, but it was Clark who did the labor. His efforts were rewarded by praise in the *Mariposa Gazette*, which said that he should be "commended and encouraged, as he has by his industry, rendered it perfectly easy for the most delicate female to travel without fear or danger."

Files of the *Gazette* are gold mines of information as to the rough-and-ready doings of Galen Clark. He was a friend of successive editors, presenting them with news, venison, and bear meat on his frequent trips to Mariposa. In turn they reported favorably, if grandiloquently, on his activities, as well as those of such Yosemite Valley pioneers as James Hutchings, James C. Lamon, and Stephen M. Cunningham.

Those three were also involved with terrific storms. Lamon was an eyewitness to the Valley's flooding, and the aftermath of uprooted trees, debris, and sandbanks. Beginning in 1862, Lamon, who raised apples and berries on land he preempted in the upper end of the Valley, was its first permanent, non-Indian resident. However, Cunningham and an unnamed friend had spent the 1856-57 winter there, blocked by heavy snow but befriended by Indians.

In May, 1864, Galen build another small windowless log cabin, this one at the Mariposa Grove, for a shelter. Soon after it was finished, a party of New Englanders took refuge in it during a thunderstorm, and one of them

promptly named it "Galen's Hospice." Among the people of distinction Clark met were Jessie Fremont, Horace Greeley, California State Geologist Josiah Whitney, Thomas Starr King, and steamship magnate, Israel Ward Raymond. Not only did Clark provide them with shelter and food, but guided them through the Mariposa Grove and often into Yosemite Valley.

His love for those places and his concern for their preservation showed in his words and actions. Man-caused fire was a great menace as were axes used indiscriminately by hunters and homesteaders. In Yosemite Valley, stock roamed the former realm of Indians and wild animals. A cow's lowing was as common a sound as a coyote's howl. Deer and other natural game became scarce as rifle shots echoed between canyon walls. Inevitably, every homestead effort was bent toward attracting tourists and making money from their visits. Hotels, toll trails, and toll ferries represented private enterprise.

Clark spoke of the need for safeguards, and his quiet influence and the alarm of other far-seeing citizens culminated in a bill introduced to the United States Congress by California's Senator John Conness on March 28, 1864. Conness cited "gentlemen of fortune, taste, and of refinement" as the proponents of the history-making act. Undoubtedly Reverend King, who died in 1864,

Landscape architect Frederick Law Olmsted, famed for his design of New York's Central Park, had the vision and ability to organize plans for the limited development of the Yosemite Grant. (YNP Collection)

Whitney, and Frederick Law Olmsted were among such gentlemen, and Clark, himself, had influence on them. In his 1880 Reminiscences, Galen said that Jessie Benton Fremont and I.W. Raymond had been "the most active workers" for passage of the act. Raymond did more than talk; he gave Conness a set of the Yosemite photographs taken by Carleton Watkins, and those splendid views were worth thousands of words in showing why preservation was required.

The historic bill provided that Yosemite Valley and the Mariposa Grove of Big Trees, though separated by thirty-five miles, were to be granted to the State of California ". . . with the stipulation . . . that the said State shall accept this grant upon the express conditions that the premises shall be held for public use, resort, and recreation; shall be inalienable for all time . . ." Congress ordered that the Grant's 20,000 acres be surveyed, and the Governor of California appoint an eight-man Board of Commissioners to manage the Yosemite Grant, serving without compensation.

On June 30, 1864, President Lincoln turned aside from the sorrowful tasks of the Civil War to sign the bill. Official State acceptance could not be effected until April, 1866, when next the Legislature met, but on September 28, 1864, California's Governor Frederick F. Low warned "all persons to desist from trespassing or settling upon said territory, and from cutting timber or from doing any unlawful acts within the limits of such grant." To carry out these orders, Low named eight prominent men as Commissioners; Olmsted, Superintendent of Fremont's Mariposa Grant; I.W. Raymond; Professor Whitney; William Ashburner, mining engineer and member of the State Geological Survey; Alexander Deering, Mariposa attorney; George W. Coulter, Coulterville merchant; E.S. Holden, Stockton businessman; and Galen Clark.

Conservation was virtually an unknown word. Yet, in creating the Yosemite Grant, Congress took an unprecedented and monumental conservationist step by granting scenic land of unequaled beauty and incalculable value to California as a public sanctuary. In effect, the first national park had been created — a living wilderness museum. Yosemite Valley and the Mariposa Grove would ever be preserved and enjoyed by citizens of the nation and the world.

Landscape architect Frederick Law Olmsted was elected chairman of the Yosemite Commissioners. Already noted as designer of New York's Central Park, he was in Mariposa County to manage the gold mines on Fremont's 44,386 acre estate. In addition, he had been solicited to make plans for the projected University of California campus in Berkeley, and the Mountain View Cemetery in Oakland. At forty-two, he had years of background, experience, and dedication to the evolution and management of parks, coupled with the appreciation and vision that made him the ideal man to formulate the future of the Yosemite Grant. It was his responsibility, he reflected, "to take possession of the Valley for the State, to organize and direct the survey of it and to be the executive of various measures to guard the elements of its scenery from fires, trespassers, and abuse." The Grant must be guarded, yet made accessible — an inconsistent and never-ending charge.

In the summers of 1864 and 1865, Olmsted studied and superintended the Grant from well-organized camps in the Valley and at the South Fork, a short distance from Clark's Station. His impact on fellow-commissioner Clark can be imagined. Surely acquaintance with the easterner's precepts, philosophy, and ability must have had a great influence on the conservationist-minded mountaineer. In turn, Clark shared his detailed knowledge of the region and the tradition and practices of the Indians with Olmsted.

In July, 1864, the two men patrolled a fire that threatened the Mariposa Grove. Flames burned undergrowth, but made little headway on the asbestos-like bark of the Sequoias, although one fallen tree smouldered for weeks. Olmsted absorbed everything, sifting and sorting information and needs preparatory to writing a report of management recommendations. From his camp in Yosemite Valley, he observed that campers pitched tents wherever they desired, made campfires, and let their horses and pack mules forage in the lush meadows.

Just before Congress created the Yosemite Grant, Hutchings had purchased a pioneer hotel and moved in. His story, related in his book *In the Heart of the Sierras*,

Mt. Clark, a distinctive 11,000-foot peak, and the Clark Range, were named for Galen Clark. (YNP Collection)

was that he had come to the Valley for his health, pre-empting 160 acres of land in the surety of having his claim recognized by the United States Land Office. However, he knew that no survey of the land had ever been made, and was aware of efforts to have Congress create the Grant that would stop homesteading and commercial exploitation of the Valley. A man of enterprise, ambition, and intelligence, Hutchings truly loved Yosemite and did more than anyone else to draw attention and travel to the place; but after 1866, his intent was largely financial gain.

Besides Hutchings, farmer James Lamon, hotel-keeper A.G. Black, and ferryman Ira Folsom had possession of much Valley acreage, which they developed for the convenience of the tourist trade. Their private enterprise became bitterly involved with public good once the Yosemite Grant was accepted by Governor Low, and the legal wrangle to evict them dragged on for years.

Clark's private development continued without problem, however, as his beautiful, forested acreage was not considered unique or spectacular enough to deserve State protection. When Clarence King, James Gardiner, and William Brewer came to make the geological surveys, Clark lavished hospitality and information on them. In recognition of his devotion to Yosemite, they named a singularly dramatic 11,506-foot peak Mt. Clark in his honor. The mountains it dominated later became known as the Clark Range.

His friendship with the surveyors showed in a letter he wrote to his daugther Elvira on January 5, 1865. He advised her to tell her brother Alonzo to contact Clarence King in New York about a job on a railroad survey. The letter was fatherly and concerned, but his personal news was surprising for a man who couldn't pay old debts: he was going to the Coast Range where he planned to investigate a petroleum spring.

In February, the *Fresno Times* reported on excitement over the petroleum springs, and Galen Clark was listed as a member of the Elkhorn Petroleum Company, a speculative organization that incorporated with a capital stock of $160,000. Before long the springs and company went bankrupt. Once more the perennial optimist had lost on an investment.

Evidently Alonzo Clark failed to contact King, for after release from the Army he entered Phillips Exeter Academy in New Hampshire. From family correspondence, it is apparent that there was a strong tie between father and son. In May, 1865, Alonzo wrote his aunt, Mrs. George Faber Clark, who had raised him, that his father ". . . says he hopes I will succeed in getting an education, and when my money is *all gone*, he will *try* and *help* me, but seems to be rather hard up now as he has expended so much money upon his place." Clark's mother had died that year at eighty-five, leaving Jonas a widower at ninety. Two brothers, including George Faber Clark, Alonzo's foster father, were ministers, and William Clark, Galen's "bank," was a businessman, postmaster, and state senator in New Hampshire.

No dissent was made by the other Commissioners after Olmsted read his report of recommendations to them at an August, 1865, meeting, but it was not printed and may have been purposefully suppressed by Whitney and Ashburner because they wanted priority for their State Geological Survey over the Yosemite Grant. Only a portion of his concepts saw print in 1868, and the nearly complete text was not unearthed and published until 1952. ". . . Olmsted's expression of ideals of management and use," his biographer stated, "anticipate in almost every detail the fundamental ideals of the present-day National Park Service."

His leadership and guardianship of the Grant ended in October, 1865, when he returned east for new duties with Central Park. He was not replaced until several months after the Grant had been officially accepted by California's Governor Low. On May 21, 1866, the Yosemite Commissioners met in San Francisco and

> Resolved that Galen Clark be appointed Guardian of the Yosemite Valley and Big Tree Grove with power to appoint a sub-Guardian of the Valley, and that the combined salaries of said Guardian and sub-Guardian be *five hundred* ($500) dollars per annum from the first day of July next.

Clark's qualifications for the position were his thorough knowledge of the area, his familiarity with residents and problems, and his love for its unsurpassed natural features. His grasp of a guardianship can only have been enhanced by his association with Olmsted. Although the salary was small even for those days, the position was a trust and honor that must have pleased him. For the first time since he had left the East, in fact the first time in his fifty-two years, his worth had been recognized, and he possessed status.

CHAPTER III

Guardian

∎

Any thrill Clark felt at his appointment as Yosemite Guardian must have been quickly diminished by his multitudinous responsibilities. An eight-page, hand-written letter of instructions from the Board of Commissioners detailed his work: No trees were to be cut in the Grant, nor were Indians to be allowed to break off branches from oak trees to harvest acorns. Campers were to be restrained from making fires in dry grass, trails and bridges kept in good repair, and more built. Clark named pioneer Peter Longhurst as sub-guardian to attend to the tasks in Yosemite Valley; he himself was responsible for the care and preservation of the Mariposa Grove, which, of course, was near his home and business. A pioneer conflict of interest had begun.

Clark, alone, had to handle the sensitive chore of placating Valley settlers, while at the same time easing them away from their land holdings. He was directed to be sympathetic and avoid troubles, yet firm enough to issue ten-year leases at a nominal rent for property Hutchings and others considered private. It was a delicate job requiring the tact and finesse of an ambassador and the subtlety of Machiavelli. If Lamon or Hutchings refused leases they were to be required to vacate, and their land leased to other parties.

In 1859, Jim Lamon had preempted 160 acres near present Camp Curry and developed it by planting large apple orchards. Although understandably unhappy at the alternative of either leasing his acreage or being evicted, Lamon was a mild man who would not have fought the changes implicit in the Yosemite Grant's establishment had it not been for the more aggressive Hutchings.

Hutchings put up the money and the mouth that led to years of legal wrangling. He was furious at the Commissioner's edict of lease or leave, though, as Clark probably reminded him, he had taken up his 160 acres in full awareness of the bill that created the grant for public good.

William Ashburner, secretary of the Yosemite Commissioners, defended their actions in an account filed November 12, 1877. In it, he stated that Hutchings had bought land and a hotel and moved in to begin hotel keeping

> . . . about *six weeks* before the passage of the . . . Act of Congress, and several months after the bill was introduced and the matter discussed by and most generally approved of by the newspapers . . . Although Mr. Hutchings only publicly laid claim to one hundred and sixty acres of land, that being the limit allowed to a single settler, he virtually claimed and endeavoured to exercise the rights of possession over the whole valley . . . he has always insisted, so far as his acts and utter indifference to all regulations are concerned, upon the rights of allowing his horses, cattle and pigs to

Aggressive James Hutchings, whose descriptions brought Yosemite Valley world-wide attention, lived there from 1864 to 1875. To benefit from winter sun, he built this log cabin for his family not far from the base of Yosemite Falls. (Hutchings/SS Collection)

A pensive Indian surveys his former domain of Yosemite Valley. The original Yosemite Indians, led by Chief Tenaya, were driven from Yosemite by the white man in 1851. They returned the next year only to be nearly wiped out by the Mono Indians after a tribal quarrel.

roam at pleasure all over the valley, to the great annoyance of those other settlers who had gardens or growing crops . . .

In 1868, a suit of ejectment was brought against the entrenched settlers by the Yosemite Commissioners, and for several years counter suits, legislative action, and bitterness demonstrated Hutchings' hostility. Despite Clark's official status as "foe," Hutchings' books mention the Guardian in kindly words so it is believed that Clark exercised his powers in such a diplomatic way that Hutchings blamed all of the Commissioners, rather than the Guardian, for his eventual eviction. However, Hutchings and his lobbyist friends were successful in defeating appropriation bills for Yosemite for four years and in so doing blocked Clark's salary. Galen nursed his grievances until 1894 when, after new provocation, he exploded in a letter printed in the *San Francisco Examiner:*

> . . . During the time Mr. Hutchings lived in Yosemite, he utterly ignored the authority of the Yosemite Commission, and refused to accept a Lease at nominal rates. He appealed to the State Legislature and the Congress to confirm his claim to the finest portion of Yosemite, but happily without success. He and his friends were so successful as Lobbyists in the State Legislature that they defeated appropriation

Bills for Yosemite and for four years there was not a dollar approximated for the incidental expenses of the commission or for the pay of the Guardian. At one time he made a violent threatening assault upon Hon. John W. Wilcox while in his seat in the Assembly chamber because he dared, in his presence, to vote in favor of an appropriation for some improvements in Yosemite and the Mariposa Big Tree Grove . . .

A February, 1872, letter of Alonzo Clark's gave his opinion of Hutchings, which mirrored that of his father:

> Hutchins [sic] . . . I see by papers has been lecturing in Boston. He is a *fraud* not a bona fide settler at all. He bought his house and claim in the valley when it was certain that it would be given to the State as public domain and the provision in the sale was he should pay $1200 for it if he could get a title, he took the place to make money by lying and creating sympathy. . .

To fight his case and Lamon's, Hutchings appeared before committees in Washington, D.C., and traveled and lectured extensively on the wonders of Yosemite, thereby attracting sympathy to himself as well as patronage to his hotel.

Clark also continued to gain recognition beyond

Yosemite. In August, 1865, for example, he guided a group of important people through the Mariposa Grove where he displayed his knowledge and love of the Sequoias, as well as his customary kindness and integrity. Schuyler Colfax, speaker of the House of Representatives and later Vice-President of the United States; Samuel Bowles, editor of the noted *Springfield Republican* in Massachusetts; Albert B. Richardson from the *New York Tribune;* Lt. Governor William Bross of Illinois; the Massachusetts Attorney General; and Olmsted and Ashburner of the Yosemite Commissioners were among the prominent tourists in the party. After Bowles' *Across the Continent,* which mentioned the Guardian favorably, was published in 1866, Clark's dedication was known to a wider public.

In his published account of the same trip, Richardson described Clark as

> . . . a hermit and pioneer of intelligence and kindness, who has turned his back on civilization, eschewed boiled shirts; and . . . pitched his tent in the wilderness . . . Long-bearded and sun-browned, he looks like a modernized Wandering Jew, and talks like a professor of belles-lettres and moral philosophy. He furnished us with bed and board. The ladies occupied straw couches under his roof, filling the house; while their banished lords slept under heaven's canopy, in the lee of a friendly hay stack, with a blanket for lodgings and a board for a pillow.

In early summer, 1866, philanthropist Charles Loring Brace visited Yosemite and afterward described the trip in a book called *The New West.* His admiration for his guide Clark increased when he saw that the Mariposa Grove was uncluttered by advertising of the kind that had haunted his journey from San Francisco. Clark explained that he had stopped store keepers from putting up signs. Clark, Brace judged, was "the modern anchorite — a hater of civilization and a lover of the forest — handsome, thoughtful, interesting, and slovenly. . . he knew more than any of his guests of the fauna, flora, and geology of the State; he conversed well on any subject, and was at once philosopher, savant, chambermaid, cook, and landlord."

Another visitor, John Olmsted, described his 1868 impressions of the landlord's domain:

> So here we are at Clark's; a ranch fragrant in the memory of all Yo-Semite travelers for its fare and comfortable rooms . . . its charming views of woodland scenery . . .
> Clark's ranch was built more for use than show, and is capable of indefinite expansion without hurting its proportions. It is a long narrow building of one story . . . about twenty by one hundred and twenty feet, with covered stoops front and rear, and doors opening on to them from each room. The west room is used

In 1888 Galen Clark was photographed standing by the sequoia trees he planted at Wawona twenty-five years earlier. (YNP Collection)

An 1866 visitor said Clark's Station was "capable of indefinite expansion . . ." (Carleton Watkins, YNP Collection)

Bridges, fences, gardens, and even the ferry boat were washed away in the flood of 1867, but beauty remained intact. (John P. Soule, SS Collection)

as an office, and a receptacle for certain compounds for the inner man; on the outside hangs the antlers of an elk . . .

The several bedrooms, opening off a narrow hall, were separated by flimsy canvas sheets, offering, as one woman guest said, "the very best magic lantern rooms" at night.

Clark's Station profited by the ever-increased travel, but as fast as money came in, he spent it on additions or improvements to the place, as well as improving the Chowchilla Mountain Road that still ended far short of the South Fork. He increased his land holdings by further homesteading and purchasing land claims relinquished by others. Mariposa Courthouse records show that he owned about 1,200 acres in December, 1868, when he was taxed $600 for real estate and $250 for personal property. During 1867 and 1868 Clark continued his balancing act of being both an innkeeper and Guardian. Writing letters and reports to his fellow Commissioners, drawing up leases for concessionaires, attending meetings, and arbitrating problems between the competitive businessmen made up a large part of his job. Outdoor supervision was more to his liking. He superintended the building of bridges at the foot of Bridalveil Meadow and across the river above Vernal Fall, and saw that trails were improved. Despite these positive moves, the Board of Commissioners was under frequent criticism for not doing more in the way of issuing books and maps and managing the areas. They were hamstrung by the California legislature's continual refusal to appropriate funds for maintenance, improvements, or the Guardian's salary. To sustain Clark, the Commissioners voted some money from rents collected from the Valley hotelkeepers, but the legislature was so niggardly that complaints continued against the hapless Yosemite Commissioners who blamed Hutchings for the impasse.

Fortunately, the Mariposa Board of Supervisors took their responsibilities for the Chowchilla Mountain Road seriously enough to appropriate funds to repair 1868 storm damage. In February of that year the *Mariposa Gazette* reported that the Supervisors had ordered $350 to be drawn for Galen to build a new bridge across Big Creek. On March 14, the *Gazette* contained the surprising news that Clark had rented his hotel on the South Fork to Samuel Miller, a guide and ex-miner, so that Clark could stay in Yosemite Valley to pursue his guardianship cares.

He was at Clark's Station off and on during the year, however, which in early months featured damaging winds, rain, and snow. Alonzo relayed the news to his aunt:

Heard from Father —he has had his land all turned bottom side up from the floods, some of his fences have washed to the ocean, a great tree was uprooted and fell onto his house crushing quite a large part of it and now he has leased it for two years I believe and if he had

any money to pay debts would come home.
Am thankful I was born under a different star.

Yosemite Valley had fared even worse, with high water flooding parts of it and washing away bridges, including the new one. Even though trails were still blocked by deep snow, Clark felt he must take an inspection trip, and his account of it, published in the April 17 *Gazette*, demonstrated both his hardihood and sense of humor:

> . . . I started from Clark's Ranch . . . on the 30th of March at 4 o'clock in the morning, provided with a blanket, two days' provisions, a Wand, and a pair of snowshoes made after the form of the Canadian shoe, and covered with canvas . . . These shoes are awkward for a novice, requiring great care in walking or a person is likely to trip and go headlong into the snow with much more certainty than an experienced mustang could send him.
>
> While crossing Alder Creek on a convenient log, the snow-covered bank treacherously gave away and let me drop into the water below — causing me to get all wet. Here was an emergency in which I made use of my Wand. This Wand is an invention of scientific men and is much in use by many of them in their various occupations. It is a hollow cylindrical glass instrument contracted at one end which is arranged to open and close at will; it is prepared for use by filling it with a liquid somewhat like the spirit level . . . The small end is opened and placed against the face just below the nose with the larger end elevated whilst a person takes an elevation. Its influence is magical and inspiring, causing a person to see his way clear out of difficulties and into them with greater facility.

Neither the snowshoes nor the whiskey-filled "Wand" saved him from another fall. "I was not personally very injured by this perilous feat of backsliding, but finding a horrible rent in my pants something like a flag of truce hanging at half mast in the rear, I felt somewhat 'embarrassed.' A convenient sail needle and twine mended the breech."

At Summit Meadow, he found snow eight to ten feet deep while only the chimney top showed above the snow at Ostrander's sheep cabin. A wolf rushed out of the opening beside the chimney, astonishing Galen, who was rifle-less. ". . . I heard a dull thumping sound something like the drumming of a pheasant. I soon found this was caused by the 'beating of my heart' against my ribs . . . I then took an observation with my Wand and was right again." After spending a night in the cabin, he made such slow progress through soft snow that it was evening before he arrived at the Hutchings Hotel where the Hutchings family made him comfortable for two days. Hutchings told him snow had piled six feet deep in

James Lamon, a pioneer Yosemite settler, planted large apple orchards on 160 acres near present Camp Curry. (YNP Collection)

Lamon's log cabin was shadowed by North Dome in the eastern end of Yosemite Valley. (John P. Soule, SS Collection)

A flood in 1867 removed the pioneer bridge near Hutchings' hotel, but the building survived in altered form until 1941. (YNP Collection)

mid-March, and was succeeded by almost that much water when the Merced overflowed its banks. His bridge had been swept away, his orchard inundated, garden covered, and both his home and hotel encircled by the flood waters.

Clark surveyed the damage, then described it:

> All the bridges were carried away . . . the fences are mostly washed away . . . the ferry boat has gone altogether with the tree to which it was fastened . . . Heavy drifts of timber and rocks have come over the falls; large trees broken, battered and shivered like pipe stems . . . Huge boulders rolled around and piled up like a boy would play with marbles. A large number of trees in different parts of the Valley are torn up by the roots . . . enough to make a million feet of lumber . . .

For all its storm-tossed appearance, he observed, . . . a few early flowers . . . the buds of deciduous trees and flowering shrubs . . . swelling, giving evidence that the Valley is about to adorn herself in her usual new robes and put on her best flowery smile for the reception of visitors . . .

> It is a great pity that this wonderful place could not have been kept sacred and 'inalienable' for the wise purpose for which it was donated and none of it given to private enterprise. Here, clustering around are all the varied elements and romantic scenery of a continent; here are gathered in one grand focal center types of nearly all the world's most magnificent wonders . . . If gold will satisfy these claimants, I hope our next legislature will be wise enough to give of it, till both they and justice are amply satisfied thereby securing this most magnificent donation of Congress with all its varied beauties 'free' to our posterity and the world forever.

Despite a lack of funds to make improvements, and not being backed with the force that would have insured a more effective regime, Yosemite's first guardian possessed enough spiritual insight and moral fiber to match the Grant's purpose and the Valley's rock-ribbed grandeur.

CHAPTER IV

Two Mountaineers

∎

It was July, 1868, before Clark had the plank skeleton of a new bridge across the South Fork and could begin repairing the trail on into Yosemite Valley. According to the *Mariposa Gazette*, townspeople raised about $100 "to assist in this public enterprise," but most of the labor was Galen's. Despite obstacles, regular travel had begun in mid-May, and soon thereafter, a man afoot with intense blue eyes and a shaggy appearance stopped at Clark's Station. Like Clark, the stranger was to be ever afterward absorbed and involved with Yosemite and its development into a national sanctuary.

John Muir, Scotland's gift to America, was an ingenuous, questing man with a passion for botany that had carried him from Wisconsin to Florida where malaria bedded him, and on to California where he sought health and adventure. After exploring and delighting in Yosemite Valley, he and an English shipmate set out for the Mariposa Grove with the inevitable wayside stop at the South Fork. There Clark served them with mountain talk, trail advice, flour, sugar, and tea. Muir refused an offer of some fresh-killed bear meat, but said his companion, "who complained of the benumbing poverty of a strictly vegetarian diet, gladly accepted."

Decades later, in his book *The Yosemite*, Muir paid tribute to Clark by recording the kinship that existed between the two men from 1868, when Clark was fifty-four and Muir thirty, until Galen's death. Both were exceedingly independent, intelligent, and eccentric. They shared a deep love for mountains and forests and often explored them together. "Galen Clark was the best mountaineer I ever met . . ." Muir said. For example, about a scramble up the Tuolumne Canyon from Hetch Hetchy, Muir wrote:

> I had convincing proofs of Mr. Clark's daring and skill as a mountaineer, particularly in fording torrents, and in forcing his way through thick chaparral. I found it somewhat difficult to keep up with him in dense, tangled brush, though in jumping on boulder taluses and slippery cobble-beds I had no trouble leaving him behind.

After climbing Mt. Lyell together, "when the snow which covered the glacier was melted into upgleaning, icy blades which were very difficult to cross," Muir recorded further:

> . . . Here again I, being lighter, had no difficulty in keeping ahead of him [Clark]. While resting after wearisome staggering and falling, he stared at the marvelous ranks of leaning blades, and said, 'I think I have traveled all sorts of trails and canyons, through all kinds of brush and snow, but this gets me.'

Both men shared abiding beliefs in the spiritual and physical healing powers of wilderness. Clark wrote that the pure mountain atmosphere ". . . exhilarates and

Mt McClure *Mt Lyell (south side*

The Highest Yosemite Mountain

John Muir's sketches showed Yosemite's high-country glaciers with accuracy and artistic merit. (YNP Collection)

Muir travelled light, carrying only tea and bread crumbs to sustain him on his many mountain excursions. (Theodore Lukens, Courtesy the Henry Huntington Library)

thrills through every nervous fibre of the body, and makes the old feel young again. THE BRAIN BREATHES AS WELL AS THE LUNGS!

In turn, Muir found that mountains, canyons, or glaciers not only restored his work-drained health, but filled him with such enormous vigor that a tree top could be ridden during a riotous storm, a peak assaulted in blinding snow, or a crevasse leaped. Disease, germs, frustrations, and tensions could not survive in the pure, electric air of the heights.

Both practiced outdoor idiosyncracies. As related, Clark was a hater of hats and shoes and said, "I have found that by perseverance in breathing through the nose, I could climb mountains with much less fatigue than when I went panting with my mouth open half the time. The reason is that the brain is better supplied with nerve power. . . As the air rushes through the nostrils on its way to inflate the lungs, the brain attracts and inhales electricity from it."

Muir believed in traveling light with as little as one blanket and a sack crammed with bread, tea, and oatmeal. At times, he chewed tea leaves, then swallowed water, but preferred his tea hot. On one glacial exploration, he shaved enough splinters from his sled to make a fire in a tin cup and brew tea in another cup above the tiny flames.

Since the hardy adventurers had no sleeping bags, camp stoves, or dehydrated food —much less tents — cooking and bed-making were chores necessitating care and skill. Ruefully, Muir disclosed:

> In cooking his [Clark's] mess of oatmeal porridge and making tea, his pot was always the first to boil, and I used to wonder why, with all his skill in scrambling through brush in the easiest way, and preparing his meals, he was so utterly careless about his beds. He would lie down anywhere on any ground, rough or smooth, without taking pains even to remove cobbles or sharp-angled rocks protruding through the grass or gravel, saying that his own bones were as hard as any stones and could do him no harm.

Nevertheless, on the Hetch Hetchy trip, when they were separated by miles and darkness from their camp, Clark admitted that if he had his choice that night between provisions and blankets, he would choose his blankets.

Muir made enemies as well as admirers, particularly in expounding his glacial theories on the creation of Yosemite Valley in opposition to Josiah Whitney's belief that a cataclysm had caused the canyon to drop. For years, a celebrated battle raged between them. Clark backed neither, but quietly made his own observations, which he did not publish until 1909, by which time glaciation was accepted widely as fact.

He believed that the Valley's creation had come about by

Clark and trailbuilder Milton Mann made the effective discovery of the Mariposa Grove in June, 1857. Clark later built a stone cairn to mark the spot from which he first viewed a giant sequoia. (YNP Collection)

. . . some great subterranean force of gases or superheated steam . . . forming great dome elevations. In some instances this force was sufficient to burst open the surface and make a complete blow-out, forming a great chasm with vertical sides. The bursting open of two or more of those great domes seems to have been the original agency in the formation of Yosemite Valley. I can imagine no other theory to account for the various lines of cleavage and fractures in the great walls of the Valley . . .

However, he did acknowledge that glaciers had concluded the corrosive and sculpturing actions that made the Valley "a crowning diadem of unspeakable sublimity and grandeur."

It may be that Muir first heard of his friend's divergent conception when he read it, for the two had no known disagreements, only a genuine admiration for each other. On the whole, Muir was a merry, outgoing, and vocal person; Galen a kindly, sober, reserved New Englander. Muir had a sly humor; Galen one so shy that Muir remarked,

. . . although glances of his eyes and slight intonations of his voice often indicated that something funny or mildly sarcastic was coming . . . however deep and fun-provoking a story might be, he never indulged in boisterous laughter.

At an evening campfire in Yosemite Valley, Galen was so bombarded by requests for "big stories" about Yosemite that finally he countered quietly: "I am not a blatherskate, my good woman. I do not tell stories, but I will answer questions. I am not a spurting, gushing geyser of information. I am not an artesian well, but I can be pumped."

Muir needed considerable priming from friends

Clark, pictured here in the Mariposa Grove, and his friend John Muir were both tree lovers, awed by the grandeur of the massive sequoias. (SS Collection)

before first writing and publishing his thoughts. Thereafter, however, he needed no "pumping" to launch into speech or print, which he did with great frequency, wide circulation, and impact. Sometimes his adjective-laden prose was extravagant, but much of it is still read, quoted, and remembered. One of the most memorable and appealing of his passages is his exclamation:

O these vast, calm, measureless mountain days, inciting at once to work and rest . . . Nevermore, however weary should one faint by the way who gains the blessings of one mountain day: whatever his fate, long life, short life, stormy or calm, he is rich forever!

Galen's articles for the *Mariposa Gazette* and the *California Farmer* were more pedestrian and less-read, but nonetheless heartfelt. In his *Gazette* letter of April,

1868, he wrote eloquently and lovingly of Yosemite Falls:

The Falls are now at their middle volume of water, beautiful as ever, whitening as they make their careless leap over the great perpendicular height, widening and involving into a thousand magical and fantastic forms of beauty; silvery falling rocks and meteors, softening into folds of lace and misty gauze ever disappearing into the cauldron of water and spray beneath.

Beyond their writing, the two mountaineers are remembered for the loving and thoughtful care that went into Clark's official guardianship and Muir's unofficial guidance which kept Yosemite inviolate and its visitants "rich forever."

CHAPTER V

Two Hats

∎

After the driving of the last spike on May 10, 1869, America's thirty-seven states were truly united by the transcontinental railroad. A dramatic increase in tourism was anticipated by California businessmen including those in Yosemite. By trial and error, James Hutchings assembled a water-powered sawmill, and then hired John Muir as "a good practical sawyer" to run it. As fast as Muir cut lumber, carpenters utilized it. Hutchings wrote, "The old house was rejuvenated by porches, and made convenient by lean-tos . . ." The biggest improvement was the installation of walls and doors to replace the former, flimsy partitions of cloth. No longer would privacy be non-existent and husbands separated from wives as, before that, women had the upstairs rooms, men the down. Even after the additions of kitchen, store, and sitting room, beds were only available for twenty-eight guests. Rarely were they all filled, but one chaotic night, blankets had to be spread on the floor to accommodate a total of fifty-seven people!

Alex Black reassumed management of his barn-like Lower Hotel, which had been leased to Isabella and George Leidig, tore it down and built a larger shed-like affair. Promptly Leidig applied to the Yosemite Commissioners for permission to build a new hotel near the base of Sentinel Rock.

Encircling porches on the ground level and second floor gave the large, shake-roofed building some architectural merit. The other exciting 1869 event for the Leidigs was the advent of son Charles, the first white boy to be born in the Valley. Lively, five-year-old Florence Hutchings had been the first white child born there.

Charles Peregoy had a cattle camp at a 7,000-foot-elevation meadow halfway between the Valley and the South Fork. In 1869-70, he enlarged his log cabin so it would accommodate sixteen guests although often more crowded in. Still another hotel was build by Vermonter Albert Snow on the flat below Nevada Fall.

Innkeepers' efforts were rewarded when visitation to Yosemite Valley almost doubled — 623 to 1,122 between pre-railroad 1868 and 1869 — and, after that, travel increased by two hundred or more each year until 1873. Thanks to the journalistic efforts of visitors, it is known that Mary Peregoy made cream pies fit for the gods, Emily Snow's doughnuts, baked apples, and baked beans were incomparable, and that Belle Leidig provided "choice viands" including ice cream.

Presumably, the oft-changed cooks at Clark's Station produced less memorable meals, for none were recorded in travelers' records, but a *Mariposa Gazette* reported that no one at the inn had to live by bread alone.

A pack train went through on Tuesday for Clark's on the South Fork. From the individual appearance of the packages, bibulous individuals can be accommodated . . . cases of wine,

Lumber from the sawmill run by John Muir "rejuvenated" Hutchings' Hotel with porches and lean-tos. A kitchen added to the back surrounded the cedar tree that towers above the structure. (SS Collection)

The kitchen was eventually turned into a parlor whose focal point (the large cedar tree) survived seventy-five years of incarceration and is still alive today. (YNP Collection)

cases of whiskey and brandy, largely outnumbered the packages of more substantial grub.

In 1868, Clark again rented his place to Sam Miller so that he could be free to guard the Yosemite Grant. Sometimes his "two hats" were one as on an April, 1869, trip to the Valley when his survey of trails and winter damage was a Guardian's task, but one a hotel keeper benefited from too. Again, a letter of his in the *Mariposa Gazette* informed readers of Yosemite conditions.

> I made the trip on foot in one day. The Valley has sustained no damage by the storms of the past winter, except the breaking down of large quantities of branches . . . Mr. Lamon has been getting out material for a two-story hewed log house and making a line fence around his line boundaries . . . Mr. Hutchings is enlarging his strawberry grounds . . . Fred Leidig and wife are making good preparations to entertain visiting guests . . . I enjoyed their kind hospitality . . .

After that, Clark made his headquarters at the Leidig Hotel rather than at the Hutchings' House, a diplomatic move since one of his responsibilities was to rid the Valley of settlers such as Hutchings. In June, Clark appointed Leidig sub-guardian of Yosemite Valley. Both Lamon and Hutchings had had their claims located, surveyed, and marked off "last fall by the State Surveyor General . . ." Clark wrote, "Whether they will be permitted to hold their claims in accordance with this survey remains yet to be decided . . ."

That fall a heavy acorn crop precipitated a touchy public relations problem for him to arbitrate. Acorns were the staff of life to Ah-wah-nee-chee Indians, who stored them in chuckas for future use in making bread, meal, or flat cakes. It was their custom to break laden branches from trees. Clark's task was to persuade them not to injure the trees, but to wait until the crop fell naturally.

Indignantly, the Indians argued that Ahwahnee (meaning deep, grassy valley) — was *their* Valley, that they had never been paid for it after the Mariposa Battalion had seized it in 1851, and therefore they could do whatever they wished to *their* trees. Clark countered that the Valley was now owned and protected by white men and no one, red or white, was allowed to harm the trees. The Indians scoffed, but because of their mutual respect he eventually won a grudging promise that the branches would not be broken. Another Indian tradition was their practice of emerging from steaming sweat houses for immediate plunges in the river. After a diphtheria epidemic had weakened them, such immersion was suicidal, and when measles spread in the state, Galen talked them into discontinuing this custom.

White men, too, encountered his sober speech, and in January, 1870, his righteous wrath when he caught the men responsible for cutting a huge pine near Hutchings' Hotel. They were fined $20 each by a Mariposa judge.

Leidig's Hotel was far from luxurious, but the surrounding landscape made guests happy. (SS Collection)

Black's Hotel, built in 1869, was torn down in 1888. The lumber from its rambling walls was later used in the construction of the "Kenneyville" property, which stood on the present site of the Ahwahnee Hotel. (YNP Collection)

While succeeding as Guardian, Clark continued to fail as a hotel keeper. Because of weather and roads, the tourist season was limited to a few months, and he could not devote the necessary time to his place. He had borrowed money to build a wagon road and improvements on which he did not realize an equal cash return, and he had too many people on his payroll. By 1871, no less than eleven men worked for him. In the summer, extra help was needed for milking, haying, butchering, shoeing horses, and other ranch chores.

At least one-third of Yosemite's visitors came and went on northside horse trails, not even approaching Clark's Station. In 1868, six to eight hundred of the over 1,100 visitors stayed at Clark's during a six-month period. Obviously, the house count and cash received could not have been munificent. Furthermore, Clark's charges for lodging and food remained modest, help was expensive, and he lost on debts. His extensive acquisitions of surrounding acreages had made him land rich but money poor.

On December 7, 1869, he sold an undivided half interest in his acreage, the hotel, its furnishings and the toll bridge across the South Fork to Edwin "Deacon" Moore for $2,000. A rancher named Henry S. Rockwell put up half the amount, but he was a silent partner. After a bitter campaign, the previous fall, Moore had lost his office as County Recorder by only a dozen votes. During his four-year tenure, he and Galen had been friends and associates in a turnpike company. Like Clark, Moore was a great favorite of the *Gazette's* editor, who lauded him in print as earnest, straightforward, and honest, hence, perhaps, the cognomen "Deacon."

Moore, an amiable but restless man, had been born in Ohio in 1821 and came to the Mother Lode in 1849. He next kept a hotel in Central America, and then mined in Australia before returning to Mariposa County where he was a miner until elected Recorder. He married Ohio-born Huldah Traxler in 1866.

In his 1880 Reminiscences, Clark claimed that he had taken in Moore "as I wanted a partner who had a wife."

However, an 1870 letter of his to a niece revealed the painful truth. "I sold a half interest in my place to raise money to pay off some indebtedness incurred in building." Moore was conversant with Clark's land mortgages. An 1867 one for $600 had been repaid, but another for $1,500 at 2 percent interest per month was still in effect when they became partners.

An early May *Mariposa Gazette* reported that the Moores had gone to the South Fork, "to a happier land." There travelers were to gain rest, savor speckled trout, and receive unexcelled hospitality under the management of Clark and Moore. Clark told his niece they were making many new additions, "among other buildings, a sawmill in order to get lumber more easily for more necessary improvements. All our other . . . buildings have been made by working the lumber out of trees by hand. We are just now getting fixed to make money another season if we have a good run of business which now there is a good prospect of."

As ever, Galen was gambling labor and money on a rosy future; as ever, he was optimistic, but this time his vision and investment were shared by Moore, a businessman and former county official.

Most Westerners were far too occupied grubbing out land and a living to travel, but Easterners, Englishmen, and Europeans were more settled and many had money, leisure and curiousity enough to investigate the scenic wonders described so lavishly in the public press. However, they were used to smooth post roads and riding in well-appointed trains or stagecoaches. They thought

The Yosemite Indians stored their acorn crop in chuck-ahs, which they wove from willow sprouts and thatched with pine branches. (Hutchings/SS Collection)

little of California roads, and even less of Yosemite's trails, and said much concerning the heat, dust, and necessity for decent stage roads.

Clark listened, agreed, and acted as did other progressive businessmen in towns serving the north side of Yosemite Valley. He was well aware of the formation of turnpike companies in Coulterville and Tuolumne County, and felt that Mariposa must compete. In March, 1869, Clark and Moore and four Mariposans had organized the Mariposa Big Trees & Yosemite Turnpike Company to build a toll road to Clark's Station and the Mariposa Grove. Seven pages of field-survey notes were filed in the Mariposa Courthouse, but by December 17 Galen admitted in a public letter to the *Gazette* that the company had "become somewhat demoralized, and badly needed backers." His plaintive conclusion ran:

> Are the people living on the Mariposa route to Yosemite Valley willing to lose the travel rather than assist in making a wagon road further to the place! . . . A subscription paper will . . . be circulated to ascertain how much assistance will be given to the enterprise. Either money, work, or anything else which will give material aid will be most thankfully received and economically expended.

Evidently aid was not forthcoming for in February, 1870, the *Gazette* reported the organization of a new turnpike company in which the original six subscribers were reinforced by the addition of eight more Mariposans. Moore was elected secretary while Clark, who was such a failure with figures, became treasurer. Naturally, the *Gazette* had a keen interest in construction of the road that would bring more travelers through its town, and reported enthusiastically on its progress from April to its July completion when it was termed "not inferior in grade and construction to any mountain road in the State." At the same time construction was going on, a bill to finance its continuance from the South Fork to Yosemite Valley was killed in the State Assembly.

Versatile, ex-miner John Conway was the surveyor and road-builder for the toll road. Grades were steep, as 2,800 feet had to be ascended in the five miles between White and Hatch's and the summit of the Chowchilla Mountains. From that height the new route plunged down 1,700 feet in less than five miles to Clark and Moore's where it terminated. In anticipation of completion, shelter for the teams of horses had to be built, a Wells Fargo agent and express box installed, and tolls set by the Mariposa Board of Supervisors. On June 10, they fixed charges of $1.00 each per footman, $2.00 each for a vehicle drawn by one horse, $4.00 for a vehicle pulled by two horses, and on up to $12.00 for each eight-horse stage. Clark and Moore were to collect the tolls, which were sorely needed as the road had cost them over $12,000, half advanced by Clark with the money received from Moore and Rockwell, plus a loan from

Elvira Missouri Clark, above left, was the oldest of Galen's five children. She came west in 1870 to visit her father. (YNP Collection)

Clark's youngest child Mary Ann Clark Regan, above right, made him a grandfather in 1867. (Regan Family Collection)

Amiable, restless Edwin Moore, pictured at left, traveled afar before settling in Mariposa County. (Carleton Watkins, SS Collection)

Samuel Fisher of Stockton. Fisher was associated with the A.N. Fisher & Company stage line whose stages would carry passengers to Clark and Moore's. By July 23, 1870, the road was complete, and stages were raising dust on it.

Stage arrivals were invariably exciting because the passengers signaled revenue and activity for everyone involved with the hotel. No guest received more personal attention from Clark than did a trim young woman with brunette curls, resolute eyes, and firm mouth who arrived in 1870. Her name was Elvira Missouri Clark, and she had not seen her father since 1854 when she had been fourteen, nor lived with him since the age of nine. Her Aunt Clarissa and Clark's parents had given her, her sister, and her two younger brothers a home. After teachers' training, she had taught in New England, and then in Warsaw, Illinois, not far from her McCoy relatives in Missouri whom she visited in 1868. Now she had traveled across the continent to see her famed father, a man she barely knew.

They talked about the large Clark clan in the east. She gave details of Clark's father Jonas' death, at ninety-five, earlier in the year, and of her brother Alonzo, ready for his senior year at Harvard. Galen enjoyed hearing about his only grandchild, daughter of Mary Ann Clark Regan and her husband. Later a boy named Harry Clark Regan completed the family.

Elvira probably told Clark of his brother William's misfortunes; if not, William's daughter, Clara, had done so in a letter urging Uncle Galen to repay some of the money William had loaned him over the long, lean years since 1837. Clark's December, 1870, reply was one of earnest embarrassment, reminiscent of his Missouri communications:

> In all my various undertakings, I have had but one object in mind and that was to save money to pay off my indebtedness to my friends, and I still work in hope of soon being able to do so. I have never been well in the last fourteen years and am not able to do hard lifting work . . . If your father has known what it was to be unsuccessful in business with his superior business faculty, I hope he will in some degree excuse my inability to acquire wealth here where business is much more uncertain than in the Eastern states. I should very much like to return to see my friends once more but as yet have never been able and I never shall go until I can take money enough to pay off my indebtedness there.

Earlier in the apologetic letter, he had mentioned, "I have had much sickness and have lost much by persons owing me — in security debts and mining speculations."

By 1870 the Elkhorn Petroleum District and its ambitious plans had oozed away as had the oil springs, leaving him with little more than worthless stock. As for his health, his lungs were ever weak so colds and recurrent attacks of grippe were hard on him, but his physical activities were formidable. Conversely his business abilities were weak, for he continued to extend credit, give food and jobs to free-loaders, and even after the advent of the Moores, run the hotel business in a haphazard and incompetent way.

Despite conspicuous faults, Clark's intelligence, interests, and devotion to the Yosemite Grant continued to impress visitors. Over the years such distinguished persons as Samuel Bowles, Grace Greenwood, William Jennings Bryan, Clarence King, John Torrey, and Charles Warren Stoddard were so appreciative of Clark they sent him books or photographs of themselves. He inserted the portraits in a handsome leather album "Presented to Galen Clark by the party of April 20, 1866, as a token of gratitude for his kindness to them on their journey to the Yosemite."

That party of twelve, led by diplomat Anson Burlingame, for whom Burlingame, California was later named, had special reason to value Clark for he had been their guide, caretaker, and cheer while they floundered through snow drifts on their way to the Valley. Their arduous trip, by horse and then on foot, had been the earliest ever attempted by tourists.

In contrast to his appearance and garb, Clark's mind and library startled men like C.L. Brace, quoted earlier, and an English clergyman who spoke of Clark in a speech that was printed in a December, 1869, *Mariposa Gazette:*

> To look at him with his rough dress, rougher beard and trousers, Western fashion stuck in his boots, you might carelessly put him down for a coarse, tobacco-chewing swearing son of the forest. But take the flower of a fir cone in your hand and ask him what it is. He will give you at once its Latin name in soft measured speech, and with courteous rejoinder. He has a few books in the window of his ranch. I laid my hand at once on Goethe's Faust and Robertson's Sermons. Again and again we met with combinations or contrasts of character in the same individual which, I think, could hardly be found in the Old World.

Another admirer stated, "Place Galen Clark in any position, at the head of an army, in the cabinet, or in the Presidential chair, and he will fill that position with honor. . ." After meeting Clark, people sent him tokens of their regard — books, paintings, a handsome cane,

John Muir called the sequoia trees the "greatest of living things." The giant shown here is in the Mariposa Grove. (SS Collection)

Nonchalant host Clark watches a couple of sidesaddle visitants in 1870. Edwin and Huldah Moore stand at right under the porch roof. (John P. Soule, YNP Collection)

and a spy glass "to lengthen out the vision . . ."

On May 10, 1871, Clark and Moore made room for Ralph Waldo Emerson and his entourage of a dozen. A disconsolate John Muir accompanied the party, fuming inwardly because Emerson, his hero, had been dissuaded from spending the night with him camping in the Mariposa Grove. Early the following morning, the party set off on horseback for the Big Trees with Clark as a guide. One of Emerson's reactions was the statement, "The greatest wonder is that we can see these trees and not wonder more." Guardian Clark asked Emerson to name a giant sequoia and, after some pondering, he selected the name of Samoset to honor a New England Indian chief.

Local Indians, who had a cluster of bark shelters behind the hotel, depended on Clark and Moore for food and jobs. A number of them were employed as woodcutters, laundry and kitchen help, fishermen, and horse trainers. Probably Indians helped dig the gravity water-flow ditch whose inception was a point two miles up on the South Fork. The ditch was about four feet wide and three feet deep and supplied adequate water for both the hotel and irrigation. It was an ingenious system, surveyed, planned, and directed by Clark early in 1871.

In June, 1872, author Grace Greenwood mentioned the Indian camp where

> bloody Diggers — howling fitfully that night over the bearskin couch of a venerable savage, said to be over a hundred years old and dying without benefit of clergy, but, the next morning, the forest was again tranquil as the old chief had survived after 'teasing the affections of his heirs.'

On one occasion in 1870, the Indian neighbors were a menace to the forests that Galen had been appointed to guard, as they started a fire that threatened the Mariposa Grove. Clark and others spent four days clearing fire lines to stop the flames, which burned over a mile of their fence. Actually the Indians' traditional practice of yearly burning to clear undergrowth was good, but settlers, unaware of the beneficial effects, stopped them.

Not long after Emerson's visit, Clark was thrown from his horse and injured so badly he was "laid up" for two weeks "in misery," he said, but was cheered by the hopes of having his only surviving son visit during the summer.

CHAPTER VI

Father and Son

∎

On June 28, 1871, Galen Alonzo Clark wrote his foster mother:

> It is all over, we have graduated and are students no longer. I have my degree but have not opened it yet for it is tied up very nicely. . . . I never felt so completely unsettled as to what I should do in my life . . . I am determined to go West if it is a possible thing and see if I can find something there or on the way. . .

Harvard archives show that Alonzo, twenty-five, had graduated 98th in a class of 144, having majored in the classics. During his senior year he had been in charge of 290 boarders as steward of a College Boarding Club. From the age of four, Alonzo had been raised in the ministerial home of Harriet and George Faber Clark and thoroughly indoctrinated with the values of religion, education, and responsibility. In the 1871 Harvard Class Book he recorded: "The only difficulty I have encountered in getting an education has been that of supporting myself most of the time." To earn money, he had taught one session in a New Hampshire academy, a year of private school in Boston, and also worked at haying and book peddling.

His brief service in the Civil War had advanced his education for "I exerted myself till I got detailed on extra duty as clerk in the office of Major General Lew Wallace, at Baltimore, where I had an easy time and large pay which enabled me to go to school on my return home." After attending Phillips Exeter Academy, his entry in the Harvard matriculation book noted, "Father not responsible and letters not to be sent to him," indicating self-reliance and awareness of his father's inability to help. However, Alonzo took pride in his father's position as Guardian and Yosemite Commissioner, which he showed by mentioning it in his Class Book chronicle.

Alonzo's letters to his foster parents show him to have been affectionate, grateful, a good manager, and resourceful. On the debit side he was proud, sometimes contemptuous, and a conformist. In 1868, sister Elvira raised his Unitarian ire by uniting with the Orthodox church. "Our family seems bound to make themselves notorious by fair means or foul . . . I hardly think a person in their right mind would turn from a liberal . . . to a conservative, it seems contrary to the laws of nature." Despite Alonzo's sarcasm, the sisters and brother kept in close touch and shared letters from their absentee father. Although he had not fulfilled the traditional role as parent, they were proud of his official position and the laudatory comments they read about him in magazines and books. A mixture of affection and adventure had drawn Elvira to visit him in 1870 and again in 1871. In fact, her enthusiasm had intrigued Alonzo. "Father's place together with land he has taken up on one of the Rail Roads across the Continent will be worth a fortune in a few years," Alonzo wrote his aunt. "A fortune is not a thing . . . to . . . let slip through one's fingers . . . when it is almost in your grasp."

Alonzo sounded calculating and ambitious, yet the latter trait was a good one. Other letters note that he tired easily, slept a lot, and had trouble with his teeth. It is probable that the trip west was planned to better both his health and his relationship with his father. Alonzo left Boston for St. Louis on July 4, 1871, to visit the McCoys near Waterloo, Missouri, before journeying on. While aboard a Mississippi steamer, his watch, knife, and money were stolen, but luckily his train ticket was safe, and cousin Galen Clark McCoy loaned him $50.00.

As he had been only eight when his father had left the East, Alonzo's memories of him were fragmentary. Their reunion after seventeen years must have been formal. Alonzo studied the stalwart, compact frontiersman with gray-streaked beard, and broad, benign face and realized that his fifty-seven-year-old father was handsome. Pale, beardless Alonzo, with wispy mustache, and short neatly combed hair was far less impressive, yet his features were even, his brown eyes thoughtful, and he had a stamp of independence. Before long they established rapport, and Alonzo displayed a son's concern, telling his aunt, "Father's health is pretty good, but he works too hard doing something all the time . . ." He also showed consternation at Galen's business affairs: "Father is fearfully in debt. If persons were so disposed, I am afraid they could force a sale of his half of the place." Part of the problem, Alonzo observed, was the overhead. In addition to Clark and Moore, the partners, Mrs. Moore, and "Elvira who works quite well," he said:,

> There are two Chinamen here who do the washing and ironing, a boy who takes care of the cows, makes up the butter, cuts up the wood, etc., a big black cook from 'Frisco,' a clerk named George Templeton, two carpenters, a man at the sawmill besides farm hands.

Alonzo's twenty-five preserved letters are of great value to Yosemite historians, for they contain descriptions of a pioneer inn as well as candid observations about well-known people and places. Although his punctuation and paragraphing are eccentric at best, his text is lively, and he, himself, endearing. He signed them Galen A., or G. A. Clark, but was called Alonzo.

A few days after his son arrived, Galen guided him and some visiting congressmen through the Mariposa Grove. Alonzo was impressed with the venerable sequoias and the fact that "the one called Andy Johnson, which had been inclining gradually for a year or two to the *South*, lost its balance a few nights ago and fell with a fearful crash . . . distinctly heard five miles away."

In late August Alonzo was treated to a trip into the famous Yosemite Valley led by his experienced father. ". . . Elvira on the old mare. Father and I . . . on colts, hardly broken . . . following a blazed trail winding

Harvard graduate Alonzo Clark was footloose but ambitious when he arrived at Clark and Moore's in August, 1871. (YNP Collection)

around the mountains, up hill and down, through heavy timber . . . across little streams . . ." until they reached Peregoy's, a splendid dinner, and an overnight stop. Wallpaper, he mentioned, had been put on the cloth-lined log walls, but "the ceiling of cloth flops up and down when the wind draws through." Galen showed him the Sierra ". . . high snow clad peaks and towering above all the rest in sight was 'Mt. Clark' named after my pere by the Geological Survey.

"Next morning after a four-mile ride we came out of the timber and onto a precipice and there the valley was under our feet . . . This was the grandest view I ever had seen." From Inspiration Point they descended ". . . the steepest roughest road I had ever seen. Father and I walked to relieve the horses, at first it was very easy, but before we reached level ground my knees were so weak I could hardly stand. The trail was very dry and dusty and I found California dust to be very penetrating . . . dust worked in around the [boot] soles so my feet were black."

Alonzo soon discovered that his father, pictured here in 1886, was "fearfully in debt." (I. W. Taber, SS Collection)

En route to Yosemite Valley, the three Clarks spent a night at Mary and Charles Peregoy's pioneer inn near present-day Bridalveil Creek Campground. (SS Collection)

From old Inspiration Point, situated above the present tunnel, Alonzo had his first glimpse of Yosemite Valley. (Dean Shenk, 1979)

Yosemite Valley awed Alonzo as it still did his father, who guided them through it, took them to watch a sunrise at Mirror Lake, and then up to Vernal and Nevada Falls and into Little Yosemite Valley. They spent two nights at Leidig's Hotel, had ". . . all the fruit and berries we could eat . . ." at Lamon's, met the Snows, ". . . his is the house of a wise man founded on a rock, situated on a bank between the foot of Nevada Fall and the top of Vernal Fall . . ." returned to Peregoys and arrived back at Clark and Moore's before September first.

No sooner had they returned than travelers arrived seeking a guide to the wonders of Yosemite Valley. G.A. Darwin, Charles Darwin's eldest son, was in the group with a letter of introduciton to Galen, who elected Alonzo to do the guiding. Alonzo must have enjoyed talking to Darwin's son as he owned a copy of the controversial *Origin of the Species.* At any rate, Alonzo's journey home, September 8, stimulated him physically. "I rode 25 miles on horse back . . . over a very rough country which shows that I am much stronger than when I came here." After thanking his uncle for paying his insurance premium, Alonzo concluded the letter, "of the future I try to take no thought for this fall and winter I'm devoting entirely to getting strong."

Later Galen wrote Harriet Clark commenting that Alonzo had seemed unwell when he had first arrived, that "very little exertion tired him and he had a great propensity for sleep. He would sleep nearly all the time while here with me, at least fifteen out of the twenty four unless called up." Even though he put on weight and had a healthy look a little later, he still "seemed all the time like a person exhausted and tired out and desired nothing as much as rest." He had little time to rest, however, as Clark was so eager to share sights with him before winter that they were almost constantly on the

go. Mountain life had restored Clark's health, and he probably thought it would do the same for his son. A September excursion to Tuolumne Meadows, where they climbed Mt. Dana, and rode down to Mono Lake, was restorative. Afterward, Alonzo reported jubilantly to his aunt, "We returned home . . . sunburned, strong, and hearty with tremendous appetites, nothing so good for that as camping out in the mountains."

Eight men, including Moore and a Boston publisher, John B. Tileston, had spent $120 on food during the 19 day trip. Tileston, also writing home, described his companions as "rather a rough set, but not unpleasant . . ." He liked Alonzo and found Moore "very pleasant and ready to do anything for me." Furthermore, Deacon was jolly and swore "sparingly though he often strengthens his language in that way."

Four days after Alonzo's return, he set off again, this time with his father on a trip to pick fruit for canning from Lamon's orchards. Next the two made a trip to collect pine-cone seeds for the Agricultural Department, and late in October, visited the Fresno Grove of Big Trees. That trip, Alonzo said,

> was to get bark of the trees to sell and give away. We packed four horse loads of thick bark back home, some of it 20 inches thick. While there at the Grove we had the first rain of the season mixed with a little snow. We camped under one of the big trees which had fallen and was burned away on the lower side leaving a roof 12 feet high. Setting up long pieces of bark on one side and keeping a good fire burning on the other, we made a nice warm camp.

Clark must have been proud, not only to show his son the grove he had discovered, but to exhibit his skill as a woodsman and camp-maker. By principle, he was against injuring the sequoias in any way, but did remove bark from fallen trees.

Another section of Alonzo's long, descriptive October 31 letter demonstrated the regard that had sprung up between father and son and signaled a new era for Clark and Moore's.

> Father has made me a good offer and the chance is called an excellent one, he gives me one half his interest in the place, there are to be 4 of us in partnership, Father, Deacon Moore, Rockwell and myself, each to have 320 acres of land, the surveyors began work today, and we go into cattle, lumber, farming and hotel business the improvements mostly put up within a year are valued at 12000. These improvements with the carriage road have created a due of about $5000, which we hope to clear off next season if travel is good. They want me to look after the house and the tourists. I think it is the best thing I can do for it gives me a good honor and a good start in the world. You must not think you have lost me, for it is only a few days ride and in two or three winters I shall be East to see you . . . While about home here, I am burning stumps near the house and helping clear up so that we can fence in the house and have a green lawn in front . . . In a few years this can be made a beautiful place.

Hitherto Henry Rockwell had been a silent partner with Clark and Moore, but in November, 1871, he sold his ranch near Mariposa and moved to the South Fork inn to take an active role in its management. The first move of the new firm, Clark documented later, was to deposit "money with the United States Surveyor-General in San Francisco to pay for sectioning said township."

Before long, Alonzo became the bookkeeper for the four-way ownership, and zealously applied himself to reducing overhead. By December 5, 1871, he boasted,

> I have succeeded in getting them to discharge a lot of superfluous help. They had been paying $265 per month. We now keep a carpenter who is working on the new house $80 and a celestial cook $30. Everything has been 'running at loose ends' as they say and they must have made lots of money to have kept along as well as they have while laying out so much for improvements.

Although the busy tourist season was over, no one was idle at Clark and Moore's. "I'm working at a new job now, digging a cellar," Alonzo recorded on December 23. Deacon and Rockwell run the sawmill and I do the odd jobs." That meant helping remove storm debris from the road, blasting a rock, tacking up cloth lining in the new house, and helping in the blacksmith shop.

Excursion parties from the East increased after the transcontinental railroad made the journey easier. (John P. Soule, SS Collection)

During storms, Alonzo worked "on my Bureau . . . made of yellow pine which has a very pretty grain, oiled and varnished, the trimmings are red wood and manzanita, the latter is about the prettiest wood I ever saw." He planned to make a bureau for Mrs. Moore and a large desk with drawers "to keep account books and papers in which heretofore have been scattered to the four winds." Although he didn't mention aid from his father, Galen must have given advice and shown his old cabinet-making skill. Utilizing other skills, Clark hung wallpaper over cloth lining, hunted ("Father shot a silver gray fox"), and rode to Mariposa after mail and supplies.

Alonzo disliked the prolonged December storms, the dull evenings "with a little cribbage," and the steady diet of venison ("I am sick of it"). Fortune favored them "in the shape of a heavy limb" that killed a wild turkey just before New Year's. Alonzo had "not a cent of money," so was anxious for the settlement of his Aunt Maria Clark's estate, as she had left money to him and his sisters.

Elvira was contented, Alonzo said, though she would "probably get a school in the Spring to suit her as Mr. Bolander, a friend of father's, has been elected State School Supt. . . . Mrs. Moore is a very pleasant companionable person . . . Elvira helps her do the work so is busy most of the time." In December the two women went off visiting, and a Dr. Lee drove them from Mariposa to Hornitos. After university life, cribbage in company with three, much older men must have been indifferent entertainment for Alonzo. At times their suggestions and directions were irritating to him, and his discontent was reflected in his letters:

> While I am at work I never get lonesome but . . . these long winter evenings hang heavily

Clark and Moore's expanded lodgings, shown here in 1870, can "be made into a beautiful place," Alonzo wrote his aunt. (John P. Soule, SS Collection)

on my hands sometimes and then I wish myself back east again. We used to have such lively times at Cambridge, so many classmates and so much going on that it's no wonder a fellow misses it a little, don't you think?

In January, 1872, a cattle drive over the snow-packed Chowchilla Mountain to winter pasture relieved the monotony, but after that, severe storms kept Alonzo home, suffering part of the time from painful tooth-ache. His father was far less sedentary. Several times he made the arduous trip over the mountains to Mariposa where he attended to business, visited Elvira, and served as jury foreman for a long case. Also he did what he could to influence the passage of an appropriation bill by the State legislatures to, Alonzo said:

> buy our road and build to the Big Trees & to the Valley. Everyone thinks it will pass and if it does it will put $4000 in our pockets or those of our creditors. That bill and one good season will put us out of debt on a place worth $20,000 yet for all that I am not satisfied, the change is too great for me the work not to my taste, and I can't do things as I want them for 'old age before beauty,' and there are three to one. I can do better on my own responsibility and work with more will when I work as I please.

While his father was absent, Alonzo was chief cook. "Succeeded very well," he noted, "but was glad to be relieved" by Ah Dick whom Clark brought up from

Mariposa. Clark conveyed news that a new stage line, competing with Fisher & Co., would be running to the South Fork in the spring. "Three stages a day will make it lively for us," Alonzo foresaw. Washburn & McCready, operated by Albert Henry Washburn, a native of Vermont, and an Irishman named John R. McCready, constituted the aggressive, two-year old livery and staging firm. Merced was now a station on the new railroad, and Yosemite-bound passengers would be picked up there. On Valentine's Day, Alonzo wrote, "We are working all the time repairing, fitting up and getting ready for the travel." His tooth had ulcerated and relieved him so he was in better spirits despite the "chaos and confusion" he found in the accounts. They were in the "greatest muddle I ever saw, all mixed up, half the transactions not noted down at all, the other half on a thousand different slips of paper scattered all over the place, mistakes of hundreds of dollars . . . Father. . . is hundreds of dollars out of pocket by not keeping any better accounts."

But, he continued exultantly, he had spent two days straightening out the mess of the past two years and begun "squarely in a new set of books which I had them get . . . I shall try & keep the business so each one can tell where he stands. I'm beginning to have more influence here than I had and of course that suits me." Alonzo's ups and downs were similar to those of his father. Both envisioned pots of tourist gold at the end of their rocky, financial road. Next year, next season was the watchword, and panacea for all woes and debts.

Alonzo's sense of humor livened the letter,

> . . . in tearing down some of the old house we live in, we found inside the partition walls millions of bed bugs (the first I ever saw) from venerable hoary headed old chaps down to the cunningest little shavers you ever saw. There were numbers of large burying grounds also where the skeletons of their ancestors lie bleaching, it was quite interesting thus to find a busy little world within our own house. We lifted them up gently, handled them with care and offered them as sacrifice to the manes of those they have tormented. About once a month there comes 'so gently oer me stealing' the 'wicked flea' that keeps my hands busy. I should not mind them . . . if they did not bite.

Besides flea-hunting, bookkeeping, and furniture-making, Alonzo helped burn tree stumps which cleared

> the place pretty well, & we have a fine slope from the houses of about 800 feet in width, have so much to do that I fear we shall not get the 'lawn' enclosed and grassed down for the season . . . I have a lot of painting to do yet & paper hanging besides white washing the old house all over.

Neither father nor son showed any lack of enterprise or energy in improving Clark and Moore's.

CHAPTER VII

Alonzo

∎

At 2:30 a.m. on March 26, 1872, a tremendous earthquake shook California, Nevada, and even parts of Mexico. It was centered in the Owens Valley, east of Yosemite, and the bordering Sierra Nevada was thrust twenty-three feet upward. Latter-day experts estimate that the quake would have measured at least 8.3 on today's Richter scale, a point not equalled even in the May, 1980 shakes. Lone Pine's population of about 300 was diminished by 10 percent as 29 residents were killed and 60 injured. Its sole wooden house remained standing, but all adobe buildings were demolished. The first shock was the worst, but a second after 6 a.m. was nearly as intense, and that was followed by a series of rumbling, jolting, frightening aftershocks. Damage in Yosemite Valley was witnessed by John Muir who saw a towering pinnacle crash down followed by an avalanche. Rock slides also occurred in Indian and Illilouette canyons and near Liberty Cap. "A noble earthquake!" Muir shouted, but other Valley residents were terrified and some fled to the foothills.

At the South Fork, Galen and Alonzo tumbled out of bed and ran outdoors in the moonlight, Alonzo naked, shivering from fright and cold. After ascertaining that the one-story log buildings had withstood the quake, Clark told his son that he was glad to have experienced it, as he had "always wished to know how it was himself." Alonzo did not share that feeling, and when the ground was quiet, went back to bed again, hoping the thing was over. Soon, however, an aftershock rocked them

> very unpleasantly . . . I could hear it coming like a wave, a low rumbling, then a tremble and a shake & it would go off rumbling and muttering. The earth was trembling most of the time for 2 hours, just enough to keep me frightened all the time for fear of something worse.

Again, this time after yanking on some clothes, he dashed outside and again was driven back to bed by the chill. Finally, he slept, though far from soundly, and

> . . . about five . . . a vigorous shaking woke me up. Father got up then & made a fire & I got up too, about 6ᶜ as we were going into breakfast the house was shaken up again & you could feel the ground moving.

Alonzo's anxiety was communicated only to his aunt and uncle, but his father's reaction to the quakes gained wide audience, for two letters of his were published in the *California Farmer*, which was edited and published by "Col." James L.L. Warren.* In his April letter, Clark said, "We have been having a lively time in this vicinity for sometime past in the way of earthquakes. Generally

*Its publication began in 1854 and still continues.

45

Liberty Cap, with Snow's Hotel at the base, rained thousands of tons of rocks down its west side during the great Yosemite earthquake of 1872. (I. W. Taber, Bonney B. Douthit Collection)

2 or 3 shakes in 24 hours."

After observing earthquake damage for himself, Clark described it for *California Farmer* readers.

> One prominent point known as Pelican Peak,* just back of Hutchings Hotel, fell with a terrible crash . . . The most remarkable results of the quake occurred at Snow's . . . Mr. Snow, on hearing the terrible rumbling noise preceding the shake, rushed out of his house somewhat alarmed. The night was very light and he being in plain view of Nevada Falls, distinctly saw that the water ceased to flow over the falls for at least half a minute. A large mass of rocks, which would weigh thousands of tons, fell from the west side of the 'Cap of Liberty' about a thousand feet above its base. When this mass of rocks struck the earth Mr.

*Muir called it Eagle Rock. Eagle Peak on the north side of the Valley was unscathed.

Snow says that he was instantaneously thrown prostrate to the ground . . . The earth around Snow's place is still completely covered with dust from the pulverized rocks. I think that the prostration of Mr. Snow and perhaps the moving of the main house and the wrenching apart of the timbers of the addition was probably more the result of the concussion of the atmosphere when the rocks fell then the effects of the earthquake.

In an undated April letter, Alonzo wrote, "Only think! The ground has not got settled yet, a moment or two before I commenced writing we had quite a shake, it made the old house crack and rattle . . . If things get serious I should be strongly tempted to 'vamosh' the Ranch." Like the frightened Valley Indians and white settlers, Alonzo found nothing "noble" about the earthquake or its after effects.

From time to time, Alonzo penned caustic comments about Elvira, who was receiving $65.00 a month for teaching in Mariposa. He noted that she was so popular ". . . all the scholars wanted to go to her school. She is quite a different person since she came out here . . . has grown fat and jolly. California is a great place for health . . . A Dr. Lee lately from San Francisco but now of Mariposa is very attentive I hear to Elvira. I don't think he amounts to 'Shucks' . . . E. weighs 150 lbs. S'pose if she'd marry a Dr. it would save a large bill for services rendered." By September 13, Alonzo was even more critical of his future brother-in-law. "Elvira is not married yet. I do not know why as I have not ventured to ask. The Dr. comes up about once in two weeks and spends several days. I hope she may be happy with him and my estimation of the man may be incorrect but I have my doubts about his being able to support a wife."

Despite Alonzo's skepticism, George Pierce Lee had background to recommend him. He had been born in Massachusetts in 1839, served in the Civil War, first in the Army, and later as a Naval officer on the warship *Nipsic*. During the war, he married Anna M. Studley and they had a son whom they named George Studley Lee, but she died in April, 1866. By 1871, Lee was a physician in Mariposa where he met Elvira. In September 1872, he was one of the first doctors to settle in infant Merced. It is probable that Galen approved of his daughter's suitor. In fact, a doctor in the Clark family must have seemed a comforting and fortuitous possibility, as neither father nor son was robust. "Father's health is very poor this season," Alonzo told his aunt on September 9, 1872, "but he will have nothing to say to anyone about it so we can do nothing for him. He eats almost nothing & sleeps but very little." In an earlier letter he had confided "My throat troubles me some, it gets stuffed up at night & keeps me coughing. I think it is catarrh, but I don't know what to do for it, there are a thousand quack mixtures . . ."

Beginning in April, 1872, McCoy relatives began arriving at the South Fork. After the deaths of his parents

On a calmer day, Albert Snow, his wife Emily, and their daughter relax on the porch of their hotel. (Carleton Watkins, SS Collection)

in Missouri, Clark's brother-in-law, Joseph McCoy, Jr., had moved his family to Red Bluff, California. On April 12, he and his daughter Rosemary, twenty-four, arrived and were guided to the Mariposa Grove and other scenic spots that Galen wanted to show them. Early in the fall, Leo and Galen Clark McCoy, came to visit, help with hotel work, and enliven the scene. What reactions Galen had to a houseful of young, energetic relatives is unknown, but Alonzo's earlier opinions of the McCoy cousins had been recorded. "Leo was quite a smart fellow to work and . . . a good scholar." Galen McCoy was a "steady fellow of fair education . . . and one of the best judges of stock in" Missouri. Within a few years, the McCoy brothers were to become noted cattle and sheep judges near Red Bluff.

In April, the ever-niggardly State Legislature refused to pass the bill that would have repaid Clark for his road and financed a stage road on into Yosemite Valley. Furthermore, money was not appropriated to pay him any of the $2,000 owed him in back salary as Guardian. He

could barely meet mortgage payments, and, Alonzo recorded, the partnership with Edwin Moore was deteriorating.

> Father is also dissatisfied with the business since he has been humbugged by his partner, Mr. Moore, he has decided that we will sell as soon as we can get the land surveyed and get a title to it. The money for the survey has been paid and the work partially completed but the surveyor who had charge of it is very old & very slow . . . so father has gone to San Francisco to see the Surveyor General about having another man sent up & the work completed at once.

Plans were made to sell their half interest the next spring for $10,000, of which Alonzo anticipated $3,000 to be his share after debts were paid. "On the whole," he wrote reflectively to his uncle, "I think my year here has not been thrown away although I could not be hired to

Alonzo's doubts about George Lee proved groundless.
(Regan Family Collection)

as it was ready for use, horses were harnessed, and Clark gave free rides to all Valley residents. Repeated use widened some of the trails into roadbeds, at least in the upper end of the Valley, and after the excitement, the vehicle was available for hire to tourists as a pioneer taxi. Not to be outdone, Hutchings ordered a stage to be carried in in sections, and it was reassembled in August, 1871. In 1872, to accommodate the "traffic," John Conway built a carriage road down the north side of the Valley to a junction with the trails. After that, saddle-sore tourists could transfer to the comfort of one of the two-wheeled vehicles to take them on to the hotels.

Unfortunately, none of Alonzo's letters mention his father's "taxi" or his duties as guardian. Instead, Alonzo wrote of hotel affairs with a few bitter asides at the Legislature's refusal to compensate Clark and Moore for building the stage road. He was intent on leaving the South Fork, but did enjoy meeting some famous people that stopped at the hotel during the summer of 1872. "I received a nice set of gold studs from a New York jeweler . . . in return for attentions shown him. 'On, Stanley, on' was here as well as Duke of Saxe Coburg, brother-in-law to Queen Victoria . . . 'Grace Greenwood,' 'Joaquin Miller' and other literary celebrities." Stanley was the noted reporter who had "found" Livingstone in darkest Africa and Miller, a flamboyant poet who wrote profusely about the Sierra. Grace Greenwood (Sarah Lippincott) mentioned the place in her book, *New Life in New Lands.* One passage described Clark and Moore's as ". . . a lovely, lonely primitive place, with a peculiarly peaceful, restful atmosphere and radiance . . . Clark and Moore, both very interesting men, mountaineers of the best type and very kindly."

"Though the days were warm in that charming resting-place," the author continued

> The nights were very cool; and a bright campfire in front of the hotel was surrounded to a late hour by a circle of tourists, guides, pack-mule men, and stage drivers. We took to reciting ballads and telling stores. Of the latter, the most horrible and hair-elevating sort were at a premium. There was a generous and amiable strife as to who should contribute most to the general discomfort, and produce the most startling and blood-curdling effects . . .

Asa Gray, botanist, and Thomas Scott, railroad magnate, stayed at the inn as did other influential Californians whom Alonzo planned to contact when he moved to San Francisco. "We give away . . . keepsakes to remember the trip, big tree seeds, big tree bark . . . Manzanita canes etc . . . so we get many warm friends all through the country who remember us in one way & another. I have given away two pairs of Rattle Snake rattles to be mounted for earrings, one pair for Grace Greenwood."

In October, Alonzo received money from his aunt's estate, and soon left for San Francisco. There he rented a

stay here under the present arrangements any longer than I can possibly help." He hoped to move to San Francisco in the fall to "start reading law."

At their annual meetings, the Yosemite Valley Commissioners were vexed by the same old problems — lack of money and need of roads. On July 16, 1872, they voted a ten-year franchise to the Coulterville Road and Turnpike Company with the stipulation that the road be finished to the Valley floor in 1873. Later, a one-year extension was approved. The rights granted by the Commissioners were exclusive, but the State Legislature passed an act to allow the Big Oak Flat Road Company to extend its road on into Yosemite Valley. Competition, controversy, and appeals marred the road-building efforts of the rival companies and construction crews who raced to see which road would be the first to be finished. Ultimately, in June, 1874, the Coulterville Company was victorious, opening its road one month earlier than the Big Oak Flat Road.

In 1870, Clark had had a carriage taken apart and packed in pieces onto mules for transport into Yosemite Valley. That event caused great excitement, especially to the Leidig children who had never seen a carriage. They watched, fascinated, while it was reassembled. As soon room for $15 per week and paid 25¢ a meal twice a day. After talking to a judge, Alonzo decided against studying law in favor of a business career. Until he could see Thomas Scott or Leland Stanford, to whom he had introductions, he worked as a solicitor for a gas company at $75 a month. In November, he wrote George Faber Clark, "My own health is very good with the exception of the catarrh which has troubled me considerable but I hope to cure it here . . . as soon as I find a reliable physician."

No letters exist to document Alonzo's declining health, which probably worsened in the damp, foggy atmosphere of San Francisco. It is known that he moved to Merced, another foggy area in winter, where he worked as a clerk until forced by illness to quit at the end of January, 1873. While he was in Merced, Dr. Lee, of whom he had been so critical, saw him daily. Early in February, Alonzo started for the South Fork, but even foothill Mariposa, where he was halted, had snow from a blanketing six-day storm. Alonzo wrote his aunt that he was "blockaded in a dismal town at a very wretched hotel," without medical care or "delicate" food.

It seems odd that he did not contact any of his father's Mariposa friends, or those he had made, for aid. Mariposa had a county hospital, but it was used mainly for impoverished oldsters. Judging from Alonzo's letter, no doctor nor friend so much as visited him in his hotel room. Not even the *Mariposa Gazette* reported his illness or presence in town. Although the paper did recount his father's arrival on February 11, it did not mention the principal purpose of his trip by snowshoes and horseback. Clark said later that he had never before seen so deep a snow in the mountains; it was four feet deep at the Big Creek crossing, and six feet deep on the west slope of Chowchilla Mountain. Neither a wagon nor a horse could travel beyond White and Hatch's, frustrating plans for taking Alonzo home. Clark recalled

> We had the most snow here ever known before. We were completely snowed in. For two months I had to go over the Mountains ten miles on snowshoes to go to Mariposa for our mails and see Alonzo . . . It was hard for him to be so near to us all through the worst part of the winter without being able to get home so that he might be made more comfortable.

In early March Alonzo made a supreme effort to reach home, riding horseback as far as Big Spring House, far short of the South Fork. After resting for two days, he "hired an Indian to carry me on one of his horses as far as he could go. Then I started alone. After a little the snow began to get soft & give way, every time I went through I strained my stomach." The grim letter tells of his desperate retreat back to Big Spring House where he could not eat, had no care, and "was all used up." It concluded in words that must have been heartbreaking to his foster mother, "O! I have wished for you so many times. If I were under your care would soon be well. I

John Conway, at right with Galen Clark, was Yosemite's premier trail and road builder. He was responsible for the Yosemite Falls Trail, the Four-Mile Trail, and many others. (Courtesy Sam Conway)

am very weak, and when you get this shall be better or worse."

Finally on April 11, he wrote from the South Fork,

> I am at home at last . . . The trip used me all up so I am very weak still . . . I rode horseback 5 miles to the top of the mountain, where Father met me, 1½ miles we walked over snow & the same distance on bare ground which brought us to Big Creek . . . Here Father had some horses so we rode the other 2 miles. I am much more comfortable here.

Elvira was away teaching school in Nevada City, but the Moores and Galen lavished care on Alonzo, and he seemed to improve. In fact, he was up and outdoors, Galen told his son's foster parents, "taking exercise in the warm part of the day. . . had considerable appetite and seemed to relish his food . . . [which] seemed to agree with him much better than a month ago . . . never complained of any pain or suffering except his cough which did not trouble him much except of nights . . ."

In another letter Galen reported, ". . . I think he

49

The foothill town of Mariposa offered the suffering
Alonzo little comfort in early 1873. (SS Collection)

must have been concerned he could not live long,
though he never in the remotest way ever intimated to
me the thought his sickness might be fatal . . . He
wanted me to appoint him Sub. Guardian of the
Yosemite Valley" where he planned to camp in the
summer of 1873.

However, according to Clark, Alonzo became fever-
ish, his cheeks bright red and his eyes unnaturally
brilliant.

> But he made no complaint, always would say
> he suffered no pain, only felt weak and a short-
> ness of breath . . . but woke up Saturday
> morning, the 19th, in a sweat and weak, had
> to have help in dressing and from nine a.m.
> until about 6:30 p.m. had spells of shortness of
> breath and a difficulty of breathing . . . until
> he became so weak he could no longer clear his
> throat and could not breathe at all, and died
> from suffocation.
>
> It was terrible to see him suffer and die so with-
> out being able to give him relief . . . Poor boy!
> It was hard to see him go . . . But an overrul-
> ing Power has otherwise ordered, and we must
> submit and believe that His ruling acts are just
> and right, though sometimes to our finite
> minds they seem inscrutable.

On Wednesday, April 22, Alonzo's body was buried in
the Mariposa Cemetery where a lawyer friend read the
funeral services. Evidently, the funeral was well-
attended, for Galen had a card of thanks published in

the *Gazette*, which said, "The sweet memory of all those
kind acts will ever linger with me, and be cherished as a
holy incense arising from the altar of friendship."

"His disease was consumption." So reported the obitu-
ary, but present-day medics, who studied the complaints recorded in Alonzo's letters, think it probable
that his death resulted from congestive heart failure.

During May, Galen had to go through his son's
belongings, stop Eastern newspapers, pay bills, and
write letters — painful tasks made more onerous because tourist season was hectic. There was family ten-
sion over Alonzo's small estate. William Clark thought
that Galen would be sole heir and therefore could pay
back some of the money on the long-accumulated loan.
George Faber Clark disagreed, feeling that he and his
wife were entitled to any money left after debts were
satisfied. Galen felt he had claims too as he wrote William, "I had advanced money to Alonzo . . . which I am
entitled to even if I was not his sole heir by law." The
several hundred dollars "loaned" to Alonzo had surely
been due him for his physical labor improving the hotel
and his mental anguish straightening out accounts. The
one-fourth interest in the place given him was a handsome present, but had only paper value because of
debts. Yet Galen had some justification for his demands
on Alonzo's estate. California creditors were hounding
him, the hotel was shaky, he was still salary-less, and
even had to ask his brother George Faber to pay for the
gravestone.

The erected stone reads simply, "Galen A. Clark, died
Apr. 19, 1873. AE 26 yrs."

CHAPTER VIII

Changes

■

Of Clark's five children, only the two daugthers survived, and less than two months after Alonzo's death, Elvira married George Lee. Over the years, Dr. Lee amounted to far more than the "shucks" status accorded him by Alonzo. He became a highly respected doctor and civic figure in Merced, and official surgeon for the Visalia Division of the Central Pacific Railroad. Elvira's activities are not documented, but the Lee home, on 19th Street in Merced, was open to anyone from Yosemite, especially her father.

Despite the national depression that began in 1873, records show that 2,530 people visited Yosemite Valley that year. Drawn by the Mariposa Grove, half or more of that total traveled in or out via Mariposa and Clark and Moore's. As usual the partners had to rebuild the Big Creek Bridge, strengthen the South Fork Bridge, collect tolls, improve their lodgings, and agitate for the extension of the stage road into Yosemite Valley. They paid John Conway to survey the 25-mile route, and Clark lobbied for funds in Sacramento, but as usual, nothing but oratory issued from the State Legislature. Clark's depression increased.

"The mountains are calling and I must go," John Muir wrote his sister early in September, but he did not want to undertake a strenuous exploratory trip into the wilderness south of Yosemite alone. Botanist Albert Kellogg and artist Billy Simms would accompany him, but Muir urged Clark to join as "a companion for me among the peaks and snow . . ." At first Clark's duties held him back, but finally, he consented to go. No doubt he felt that once again the mountains would restore his body and spirit.

For two arduous weeks, they ascended, descended, scrambled, and marveled, but instead of restoration, fatigue overwhelmed Clark. Muir said that after he pointed out their further way through "a vast wilderness of rocks and canyons, Clark groaned and went home."

There was no rest at home where debts had become so top-heavy that the long-threatened financial collapse was inevitable. Deacon Moore saw a future for himself by running for County Clerk of Mariposa, but was defeated by Angevine Reynolds. In addition to holding the elective office, Reynolds became owner and editor of the *Mariposa Gazette*, and thereafter, mentioned Moore and Clark favorably. Clark faced disaster with outward stoicism, lonely without the support of his children or nephews. In the early, non-tourist months of 1874, he stayed in Sacramento, again trying to influence the passage of a road-building bill. "After being loaded down with amendments," the March 20 *Mariposa Gazette* stated, it "died a miserable death." Clark's attempts for reimbursement of his Guardian's salary were equally futile.

Nevertheless, he did not return from Sacramento empty-handed, but with a wife! On March 4, 1874, after twenty-six years as a widower, he married a woman

John Muir said that after looking at the "vast wilderness of rocks and canyons, Clark groaned and went home." (YNP Collection)

twenty years his junior, a heavy, hulking, dark-complexioned native of Spain. Her name was Isabella Pearce, and on the wedding certificate she listed Sacramento County as residence. Considerable research turned up a few facts and some suppositions. Isabella was born in Spain of Spanish heritage in 1835. Obviously she emigrated to America and probably acquired, then lost, a husband by the name of Pearce. Marian Jones Goucher, a contemporary of Clark's, said that the disparate couple met in San Francisco over a crystal ball; Isabella, or Madame Solemna as she was known, practiced fortune telling. From his appearance and conversation, she doubtless assumed that the dignified, distinctive-looking Clark, with his official position and hotel, was wealthy. According to Mrs. Goucher, Isabella married Galen for his money, which, of course, was as non-existent as her skill at clairvoyance.

The marriage ceremony was also odd, for the Unitarian-raised groom, aged fifty-nine, and the presumably Catholic bride, aged thirty-nine, were wed by a German Lutheran minister named Matthias Goethe in the presence of two Anglo-Saxon witnesses. Isabella's arrival at the South Fork shocked the Moores. Her size, swarthiness, and heavily accented English marked her as foreign in an era when prejudice was part of the social sphere. Mrs. Moore was so upset, Marian Goucher wrote, ". . . she at once moved to a cabin over on the Big Tree Trail . . ." Isabella lived in the inn where she was accepted, especially by the younger set who liked to hear her talk and her predictions. After Governor Booth and the Yosemite Valley Commissioners had been at the hotel over the Fourth of July, she called Marian in, saying, "Come in, I giva you de Governor Voot, he ride on de

'orse,' and gave me a sugar horse and rider from the cake made in his honor."

In June and July, 1874, the Coulterville and Big Oak Flat stage roads opened with respective celebrations, and immediately attracted many of the travelers who would normally have come in via the Mariposa route. That was the final financial blow to Clark and Moore, and insolvency could no longer be avoided. Chief among their creditors was Henry Washburn, the ambitious and aggressive Vermonter who operated stages from Merced to the South Fork, and the saddle business on into Yosemite Valley. His goal was to build the final stretch of road that would restore and increase travel on the southside. Since the Legislature had repeatedly demonstrated negativity, he determined to fund it himself. His partner McCready had died earlier in the year, so Washburn invited businessmen William F. Coffman and Emery W. Chapman to join him and help finance the road. Construction began in December. Thereafter they acquired Clark and Moore's holdings in negotiations concluded the day after Christmas. Only $1,000 actually changed hands for the ownership of 1,200 acres, buildings, sawmill, stage road, bridge, water system, and good will; the remaining $20,000 satisfied the debts owed Washburn and others. Clark, Moore, and Rockwell's mortgage on the property was repaid January 8, 1875, just two days after the deed of new ownership had been recorded.

Washburn, Chapman, and Coffman asked the Moores to remain as managers of the hotel during the winter when it would be kept open as kind of a clearing house for the road builders. Within a few years, Henry Washburn and his brothers Edward and John, would

After twenty-six years as a widower, Clark shocked his friends by marrying a Spanish fortune teller. (George Fiske, YNP Collection)

James Hutchings, the indomitable publicist-hotel keeper, plagued Clark's guardianship for years with his constant attempts to continue innkeeping.

As secretary for the Yosemite Valley Commissioners, William Ashburner was frequently frustrated by the maneuvers of Hutchings. (YNP Collection)

assume vigorous personal management, and the renamed pioneer inn would proliferate and prosper as the Wawona Hotel. One long, low building now called Clark Cottage, remains to commemorate Galen Clark, the founder, who spent eighteen years of his life developing the area. His labor and vision, as much as his business failure, led to Washburn's later success, and Henry Washburn acknowledged that debt in many ways for many years.

Once more, Clark had failed as a businessman, but the very traits — generosity, kindness, and trust in mankind — that contributed to his failure, had earned him so much regard and admiration that there was no dishonor. At sixty, in an era where seventy years was considered a good lifespan, he was homeless, but fortunately, not jobless. If anything, as Yosemite Guardian, he was needed more than ever, for the U.S. Supreme Court had decided against Hutchings and he was nearing a predictably stormy end in Yosemite Valley. Clark would have to arbitrate. To give him clout, the Mariposa County Sheriff appointed him as a special deputy sheriff

for the Valley. Early in 1875, he and Isabella moved there.

The famous Valley was far less of a frontier place than the South Fork. There were three hotels, a laundry, stables, a brand-new schoolhouse, and the marvelous Cosmopolitan. This establishment featured such necessities as a saloon and amenities as a reading room, and — wonder of wonders — bathing facilities. Furthermore this was not a "men only" domain; a special sitting room and one of the five small bathrooms, with tubs, towels, fragrant soaps, and even sewing materials, was reserved for the ladies. All of these conveniences had been carried in on muleback. The 25′ by 80′ Cosmopolitan, and several buildings comprising Hutchings Hotel, stood between river and cliff near Sentinel Bridge. That was Upper Village. Lower Village, a mile west, was a bigger but more scattered complex. Near the foot of McCauley's Four-Mile Trail were his tollhouse, a blacksmith shop, Leidig's and Black's Hotels, each with a cluster of satellite sheds, and across from them stood stables, an Indian encampment, and Clark's new home. It was a long, narrow structure with a small front porch and a shed-roofed kitchen attached to one side. Even today the depression from a root cellar is evident at the base of a large incense cedar, which shaded Clark's house and still thrives. Not far from the rear of the house the Merced River flowed, and Yosemite Falls boomed in the distance.

That Isabella Clark was mistress of the home was attested to by a July *Gazette* article, which said:

> We learn through a correspondent . . . that the 4th of July there was celebrated in the customary manner. . . The youth and aged alike took part in the exercises . . . a march of the school children to and from the several hotels, and finally brought up at the station where the Guardian of the Valley and his generous-hearted Dulcinea reside.
> In anticipation . . . of the youthful brigade, Mrs. Galen Clark had kindly prepared a delicious lunch, spread out upon a table.

Her crystal-ball predictions won her further acceptance according to Pinkie Ross, who spent several summers in Yosemite, and reminisced that Isabella was "very popular with us young folks. We frequented her place quite often having our fortunes told which were never quite the same, making it doubly interesting to us . . ."

Late in 1874 the State Legislature had voted $60,000 for, Ashburner said, "indemnifying the so-called settlers. Mr. Hutchings claimed by far the larger portion — $40,000 . . ." but a special commission awarded him $24,000, Lamon $12,000, Black $13,000, and Folsom $6,000. The balance was returned to the State treasury. Hutchings accepted the money and made verbal application to lease his former premises, but refused to make written application or to pay for the lease-back privilege and threatened legal action to anyone who did. However, the un-intimidated Yosemite Valley Commissioners granted management rights of the hotel to George W. Coulter and A.J. Murphy.

Hutchings waged war in San Francisco newspapers and raised public sympathy. On April 3, 1875, the *Bulletin* described his return to Yosemite "to receive guests as heretofor." Clark and others tried to dissuade him but "on or about April 14, he took possession . . . and again opened the hotel." In an attempt to circumvent authority, Clark said, "Hutchings placed his mother-in-law in charge of the hotel, and he acted as agent . . ." That tenuous management ended on May 19 when the Mariposa County Sheriff served a writ of possession for the buildings and furnishings and evicted the Hutchings family. Celebration ensued among some residents who fired guns. That "indiscreet display of ebullience" was condemned in a public meeting held the same day, which was led by a visiting politician, James A. Garfield, later President of the United States, who believed Hutchings' cry of persecution.

Guardian Clark's new 10 by 30 foot home was also his office, as the sign proclaimed. (YNP Collection)

Meanwhile the irrepressible Hutchings had persuaded ever-kindly Clark to let him "store" his personal effects in a just-finished but empty building west of Clark's home. Too late, Clark learned that Hutchings had removed the telegraph apparatus, post office, and Wells Fargo express office from his hotel and set them up in the structure. Virtually overnight, Hutchings turned the place into a hotel. "In the classical language of our friend," the *Mariposa Gazette* reported, "he proposes to remain in his new abode until hell freezes over and the devil can take a trip to Yosemite on the ice." Ashburner was even less subtle in his statement: ". . . Hutchings was officially requested to deliver up the premises to the Guardian, which he refused to do accompanying his refusal by language too profane to repeat . . ."

Hutchings remained firmly in place, renting rooms, dispensing hospitality, and taking part in community activities until the end of the season. San Francisco newspapers ceased supporting him, but the *Mariposa Gazette* was charitable. "Admitting that he has done wrong," editor Reynolds said, "would it not be better to attribute his conduct to the eccentricity of his character, and remember only the good he has done?"

The Cosmopolitan was famous for baths and booze. (YNP Collection)

Yosemite Village was laid out as shown on the map below in the mid-1870's. (Flying Spur Press Collection)

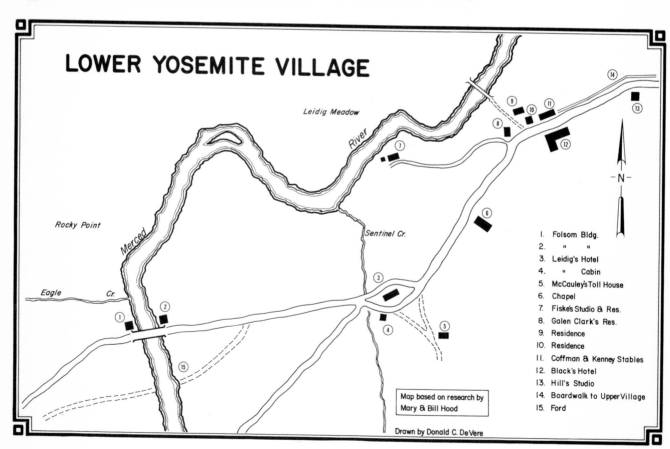

LOWER YOSEMITE VILLAGE

Leidig Meadow

River

Rocky Point

Sentinel Cr.

Merced

Eagle Cr.

-N-

1. Folsom Bldg.
2.   "   "
3. Leidig's Hotel
4.   "   Cabin
5. McCauley's Toll House
6. Chapel
7. Fiske's Studio & Res.
8. Galen Clark's Res.
9. Residence
10. Residence
11. Coffman & Kenney Stables
12. Black's Hotel
13. Hill's Studio
14. Boardwalk to Upper Village
15. Ford

Map based on research by
Mary & Bill Hood

Drawn by Donald C. De Vere

The bad he had done and the stress he had caused, plus the illness and death of Jim Lamon, undoubtedly affected Clark who, the May 22 *Gazette* reported, "is threatened with partial paralysis on the side of his head and face . . ." Subsequent issues had no further comment, but his illness may have been the reason the pioneer played so little part in the festivities surrounding the July 22 opening of the new stage road. That was the climactic event of the year, if not the decade, for just as the opening of the northside roads had begun the era of wheels, the southside road put an end to the pioneer days of travel via horse and mule.

Plans for a tremendous celebration, including a parade, bands, a program, and dances, went on for weeks under the management of five committees staffed by nearly every adult resident including Mr. and Mrs. Hutchings, but not Mrs. Clark. After Galen's years of planning, surveying, organizing, and legislating for the road, it must have been difficult for him to watch others reap the glory. Henry Washburn and partners had financed it, John Conway had been the contractor, William Coffman had the honor of driving the first incoming stage, and George Coulter, who had nothing to do with it, was the Grand Marshall. Galen's participation was limited to membership on the reception committee. Although there were several speakers, Clark was not among them possibly because of his health, but more probably by choice, for he was invariably modest and reticent.

After the dust settled, and celebrants sobered, Yosemite Valley residents settled into the routine of summer where the tourist was king, yet subject to the manipulations of men bent on acquiring as much money as possible in the short snow-to-snow season. In 1875 there was a new attraction that drew them to Mirror Lake not just for the reflection of scenic wonders, but for boating and dancing. Mirror Lake House, on the western edge of the lake, had been built by Pete Gordon, dean of Yosemite guides, and Leonidas Whorton, as a saloon in 1870. Ads claimed, "Choice wines, fine liquors and Havana cigars," as well as boats were available. By 1875 they were on the tax-delinquent list, and the Commissioners leased the place to William J. Howard, a former County Sheriff and politician. He added a 40-by-60 foot platform out over the water and built a mile-long toll road to the resort. He was also a prime mover behind the organization of a Yosemite School District and the erection of a school which eighteen children, including six Howards, attended in 1875.

Besides the ejection of settlers and the opening of the southside road, one more exciting event occurred to mark 1875. On October 12, at three in the afternoon, George C. Anderson, a powerful and intrepid Scotsman, pulled himself up onto the previously inaccessible summit of Half Dome. To achieve that feat, he had made eyebolts and spent weeks risking his life as he hammered them in and then threaded heavy rope through the rings on the final 975-foot ascent. Within a week,

Galen Clark used the ropeway and stood marvelling atop the Yosemite world. Muir made the climb before snowfall, but Hutchings waited until the following July for his first ascent.

After his controversial hotelkeeping in 1875, Hutchings reluctantly moved his family to San Francisco. There he operated a tourist agency, and gave lectures on Yosemite illustrated with stereoptican slides. As soon as the roads were clear of snow, he began escorting tourists for sojourns in the Valley and excursions in the high country.

Clark was responsible for overseeing all business concessions in the Valley to be sure that the public was well-served and not overcharged. Room and board at a hotel was $3.50, horse hire $2.50, and a guide $5.00 per party per day. Hotelkeepers, who kept a percentage of the fees, suggested that each five to six people should employ a guide. "Yosemite's not as bad as Niagara" a New Yorker judged, "but money melts very fast." To some irate visitors, weary of paying tolls for roads and trails, a guide on the floor of the Valley seemed superfluous, since there was no possibility of getting lost. Clark heard the complaints, many of which he passed on to his fellow Commissioners, tried to pacify tourists, and from dawn to dusk, answered their queries. Why were Yosemite Falls dry? Where were the bears? Which hotel was best? Where could big fish be caught?

Clark had to oversee any new buildings, check maintenance on old ones, approve expenses for state workers, answer correspondence, and prepare invoices and reports. While inspecting trails, roads, and bridges, most of which were constructed or maintained by George Anderson and John Conway, Clark was rarely undisturbed. Tourists recognized him and aired complaints. "Our stage driver should be stopped before he kills someone with his wild driving." "The guide was drunk." A few had been overcharged, fed miserable food, and made to ride lethargic mules. Hotelkeepers gave him their side, tales of petty thefts and damage by guests. As mediator, Clark listened to, and tried to appease, both sides with courtesy and dignity.

Hotelmen feuded with one another, and together railed against John Smith's Cosmopolitan, which offered not only hot baths, shaves, haircuts and billiards, but fancy drinks as well. It was fine for their guests to bathe there, but hotelmen wanted them to buy liquor at their own establishments, not the convivial Cosmopolitan.

It can be imagined that Clark faced further plaintiveness at home from Isabella as he was gone so much, and often late for, or interrupted during, meals. Nevertheless, he enjoyed the wonder in visitors' eyes and hearing them exclaim, as he repeated, "that the half had not been told them . . . for in no other part of the world can so much magnificent scenery be seen in so small a focus . . ."

By 1878, the demand for a public campground had become so great that the Yosemite Commissioners set

After William J. Howard leased the Mirror Lake House, he built a 40 by 60 foot platform for dancing over the water. (YNP Collection)

aside part of Lamon's homestead for such purpose. Aaron Harris was granted the right to administer the campground, which was near the present Ahwahnee Hotel. He sold provisions, rented camping equipment, provided some stabling, and grew fodder for campers' animals. Campers helped themselves to the abundant berries and fruit planted by Lamon.

Lamon's death from pneumonia had been a blow to Galen, for the two oldtimers had been good friends. The dead man had had only a few months to enjoy the $12,000 awarded him by the Legislature, and Galen was executor of his estate. Lamon's heirs asked him to superintend the erection of an impressive grave monument, which Conway built of three pieces of granite. That 12-foot-high marker and Lamon's still-bearing apple orchards are memorials to him.

The California legislature appropriated $10,000 for the Yosemite Grant in the spring of 1878. Such a large sum called for a policy meeting in San Francisco in May, which Galen attended. The Commissioners decided to fence 100 acres at the southern end of the Valley for the use of camping parties. Other fencing was to be repaired or torn down, and two unsafe bridges replaced. When the 90-foot iron El Capitan bridge was built across a narrow spot in the river, Clark supervised the dynamiting of the old glacial moraine, which had created a natural dam there. After that, flood waters could rush on down river instead of overflowing meadows and impeding travel. No longer was a high boardwalk needed to cross the meadow between the Guardian's home and the Upper Village, and the recurrent mosquito menace, a by-product of high waters, was greatly relieved. Although these were good effects, Clark saw that the increased flow of the river caused detrimental erosion.

Besides serving as Guardian, he was Justice of the Peace for Yosemite Valley, served on election boards, and was always involved in anything for community good. He had few idle hours during the tourist season, but winters held time for enjoyment and contemplation of the amazing natural features that made the Valley a mecca. Some of his reflections, exhibiting his ever-growing conservationist tendencies, appeared in the "Home Correspondence" section of the *California Farmer.* He described Yosemite Valley in all its seasonal beauties, noted events in the lives of its residents, and mentioned material improvements. More bridges were needed, he wrote, to "make the carriage rides around the Valley complete." During the fall and winter of 1878, visitors' animals would be allowed to run at large,

> but no stock of any kind will be permitted to . . . during the summer season. This arrangement has been of great benefit to the valley this past summer. The grapes and flowers, which were fast disappearing . . . by being closely fed by stock, have made a decided improvement which gives encouraging hope, that they will soon recover their original domain, and again assume their primeval beauty.

In January 1878, the Valley appeared "most sublime-

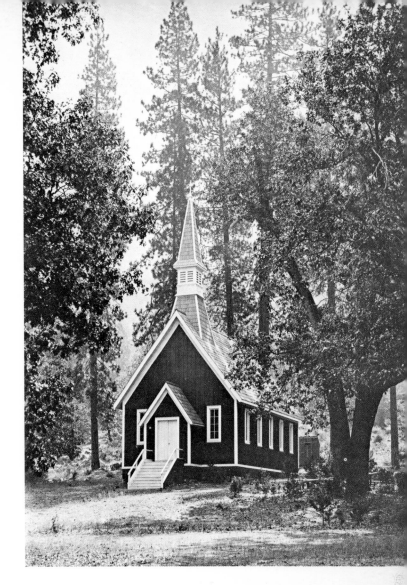

The Yosemite Chapel, built in 1879, seemed "almost like a sacrilege" to Clark. (George Fiske, YNP Collection)

ly grand in her immaculate winter robes," while its residents — ten men, three women and twelve children — cleared snow from roofs, split firewood, and cut and stored ice from Mirror Lake for summer use. The Clarks spent four winter months in Sacramento and other parts of the state, and on March 28, he reported that "I thank God I am back in Yosemite." In Sacramento, he had been so depressed by the slow workings of the legislature that

> like the youth in Longfellow's 'Excelsior,' heeding neither the counsel of friends, the warnings of the old mountaineers or the seductive pleadings of fair maidens; with a banner bearing the device 'Yosemite,' I left, and by rail, by mail coach, on horseback and at last on foot, through snow and ice, I made my way through the portals into the sanctuary of this grandest of all God's temples . . .

In another issue, Galen recorded that General Ulysses S. Grant's October visit had been celebrated with everything from powder blasts to bands playing. Also nature staged a show that thrilled Galen.

> Never before have I seen Yosemite so brilliant with the rich and gorgeous colors and tints of autumn. All the deciduous leaves seemed to assume their bright and most fascinating holiday colors, preparatory to commencing their 'death dance' in the whirling embrace of the aeolian messengers, which herald the approach of the Storm King.

Modesty was basic to Clark's character, but he was not a fence sitter. When he felt strongly about something, he expressed himself, often in print. One issue which roused his ire was the idea, fostered by the California Sunday School Association, that Yosemite Valley needed a chapel. They organized a fund-raising campaign, and construction of a house of worship not far from Clark's home began in the spring of 1879. Galen's opposition was aired in the May 29 issue of the *California Farmer*.

> It seems to *me* almost like sacrilege to build a church within the portals of this the grandest of all God's temples. It is like building a toy church within the walls of St. Peter's cathedral in Rome. But it will clearly show the contrast between the frail and puny works of man, as compared with the mighty grandeur and magnificence of the works of God, and I hope it will do good.

Although two roads completed in 1874 eased the trip to Yosemite, it remained a dusty, often dangerous journey. (YNP Collection)

59

In the mid-1870's, Clark attended a Yosemite Commissioners' meeting in San Francisco, where he had his hair cut and his picture taken by his old friend Carleton Watkins. (YNP Collection)

Earlier he had been vehement on the necessity of removing tolls on Yosemite trails and roads. Tolls were annoying and unexpected in a "free park for the world" where a demand for money caused the tourist to make

> the sudden transit from celestial to terrestrial, from the sublime to the ridiculous . . . enough to make a saint curse worse than Christ did when he drove the money speculators from Solomon's temple . . . Californians should be proud of Yosemite and no longer withhold with miserly grasp, the small amount of money necessary to make improvements and every road and trail within its limits free from tolls.

On July 5, 1879, he defended the oft-censured Commissioners:

> There seems to be in human nature, a certain amount of innate latent *'cussedness'* which ever and anon will assert its power, and give trouble to the wisest rulers, and neither the people doing business in Yosemite, or the tourists visiting here seem to be an exception to this general rule. But much has been done to improve the facilities for tourists to visit all the various points of interest; to protect them from every imposition, and to make everything pleasant for them, much has been done to preserve all natural objects from destruction or desecration.

Few criticisms were directed at Clark personally, and from the evidence, he was an able, conscientious guardian who cared for Yosemite with wholehearted love and dedication, but his term was about to end bitterly.

Chapter IX

Politics in Paradise

■

After months of deliberation, the 152 delegates of the Constitutional Convention formed a new State Constitution, which was approved by California voters and went into effect on July 4, 1879. Galen Clark had shared his doubts about it with *California Farmer* readers when he wrote: "I fear that this 'Constitutional Child' which so many have looked forward to as a 'coming savior'. . . will either prove an abortion or a monstrosity. It may be that some of the members of the Convention think they have found a 'golden egg' which by careful incubation will hatch out into a multitude of little 'golden chicks' which they may. . . divide among themselves; Quien sabe?"

Actually the Constitution was largely beneficial, but Clark had personal bias for one of the provisions was to limit tenure of State officials such as he. Among the delegates who drafted the Constitution was William J. Howard who, because his Yosemite lease had been terminated and buildings burned by the Yosemite Valley Commissioners, was vindictive. Hutchings had urged Howard to run for State Senator against oldtimer John Wilcox who was, Hutchings felt, in the pay of the Central Pacific. If Wilcox was defeated, Hutchings forecast ". . . there is hope of a new and glorious day dawning in Yosemite . . ." He wanted tolls abolished, lease times extended, and a new Board of Commissioners appointed, and may well have influenced the legislation.

After fourteen years of service, the original Commissioners were ordered removed from office, and on April 19, 1880, supplanted by a new Board composed of businessmen from northern California. Astoundingly, in September, they elected James Mason Hutchings, the evicted settler and perennial foe of the old Board, as Guardian of the Yosemite Grant. On behalf of the original Commissioners, Board Secretary William Ashburner battled their ouster and the appointment of Hutchings. For several months, Clark testified, "there was a contest between the Secretary and the people with regard to whether he (Ashburner) refused to give up his books, and the matter was carried to the Supreme Court of the United States . . ." For several months Hutchings and Clark both acted as Guardian. In March, 1881, the Supreme Court decided against Ashburner and the old Commissioners, and they disbanded.

Suddenly, Galen was jobless and faced dispossession as well, since the State owned the house he lived in. However, it was too small for the Hutchings family who were to be allowed to move back into their log cabin home on the sunny, north side of the Valley. Any fears Galen might have had of eviction were stilled when at their first official meeting, the new Commissioners resolved that "in consideration of his long services in the Valley, the late guardian, Galen Clark, should be treated with great consideration and not be subjected to any interference." That magnanimity was surprising in

TOURIST COACH

TO ALL POINTS OF INTEREST IN

Yosemite Park.

GALEN CLARK,

FORMERLY OF CLARK'S STATION,

Proprietor and Driver.

Clark's card advertised his "tourist coach," a three-seated carriage. (Courtesy Jim Snyder)

view of the previous conflict of administration, and was a testimony to the regard felt for Clark.

Furthermore, at their tumultuous June 1 and 2 meeting in Yosemite, the Board elected him sub-guardian of the Mariposa Grove, which he declined since it would have meant a move, displacing the incumbent, Steve Cunningham, and working under Hutchings. Encouraged by the fair attitude shown him, Clark asked compensation for back salary, which was rejected. Undaunted he reappeared with a claim for $750 that he had spent to make improvements, and a request for a lease on his house. Although the money was not voted, he was granted a five-year lease on the conditions that he keep it in good repair, pay a yearly rental of $1, and return it to the state at the expiration of the lease.

Assured of a place to live, Galen set about making a livelihood by driving his three-seated carriage for hire. He had cards printed that read:

Tourist Coach
To All Points of Interest in
YOSEMITE PARK
Galen Clark
— Formerly of Clark's Station —
Proprietor and Driver

His earnings must have been small, but so were his living expenses; he kept some chickens and collected and sold pinecone seeds as he had done earlier. Concern for him was expressed in an 1882 letter written by his brother Leander to William's daughter:

I had a long letter from your Uncle Galen a short time since. He says he has met with many losses of property of late and is somewhat broken down in health. He does not say a word about his wife and has never written a word to me about her. I think he got sadly taken in when he married her.

Exit Isabella. Leander's words are the last documented reference to her life with Clark. She may have left before then, though the 1880 U.S. Census indicated she was with him at that time. Why the fortune-teller left, or was asked to leave, where she went, and what she did afterward are mysteries that elude research. If she had married him for his money and position, perhaps she left him when even the latter was eradicated. Marian Goucher had a final caustic comment on Isabella: "I think he never saw the old witch again, but never did get over believing in fortune-telling and spirits."

Clark continued to be involved with the community and the county. In May, 1881, for example, he served all month as Superior Court Juror in Mariposa, and in December, officiated at a neighbor's funeral in Yosemite Valley. Visitors continued to seek him out to ask questions and advice and to take his picture. Whenever he visited his beloved Mariposa Grove, he was requested to pose for photographers, particularly in front of the Grizzly Giant and the Galen Clark Tree. After the Washburn brothers had a tunnel cut in the Wawona Tree in August, he posed time and again on the driver's seat of a stage as it emerged from the cut. Literally thousands of pictures were taken of the Wawona Tunnel Tree and broadcast throughout the world in periodicals and books and on postcards.

One of the professional photographers who settled in Yosemite Valley, after obtaining a lease to make and sell pictures, was portly George Fiske. Beginning in 1879, Fiske and his wife lived full-time in the Valley, at first in Leidig's Hotel, and later in a frame house across the road near the river. Their nearest neighbor to the east was Galen Clark, who was twenty-one years Fiske's senior. Nevertheless, the two men, who had been raised in New Hampshire towns only twenty-three miles apart, were so compatible, they became as close as brothers. Fiske took some fine photographs of his unofficial brother, and hundreds of splendid landscapes.

The death of Clark's real brother William in 1878 deeply disturbed Galen, for ever-supportive William had been only three years older than he. Galen's Sacramento stay in early 1879 had increased his thoughts of death, as shown by his article in the March 28 *California Farmer*

> The idea that I might die there, and start on my funeral tour in one of their magnificent equipages, silver mounted and plumed, and on the way get stuck in the muddy slough of the overflow, and have to be transferred to a scow and shoved over to the cemetery, at the same time that charon of heathen mythology might be supposed to be ferrying my soul over the mystic waters of the Styx, was too grave and absurd a matter for me to think of.

Back in Yosemite, the pure mountain waters and exhilarating air gave, he claimed, "new life to the weary body, and new courage to the fainting soul." Liberal use of eucalyptus pills helped him maintain vitality. "I think they are the best pills known for such disease as they are recommended," he wrote editor Warren. "They *always prove beneficial.*"

Despite his vitality, flu continued to be his yearly nemesis, and awareness of death so haunted him, he decided to prepare himself a suitable gravesite. In June, 1885, the Commissioners granted him rights to occupy his home, act as a guide, use and hire one carriage and one saddle horse, and to select a burial site. Galen chose a spot next to Lamon's grave and transplanted seedling sequoias from the Mariposa Grove to shade it. Next he dug a well and equipped it with a hand pump so he could water the trees, and then dug a wide and deep trench around the grave and partially filled it with broken glass in the vain hope that it would stop gophers and squirrels from burrowing in. These tasks were accomplished over a period of years. His obsession was well-known to observers such as Pinkie Ross who recalled:

> I was riding one day. . . by the graveyard and found Galen digging a grave. We stopped and asked him who had died. He said, 'I'm digging this for myself for then I will be sure of being buried here.'

At the 1885 meeting, already mentioned, a warrant for $750 was finally given Galen to recompense him for services and expenditures made while he had been Guardian. Fortune smiled again in December when he was appointed Postmaster for the Valley. His courteous, patriarchal manner, his benevolent expression, and correct, if wrinkled, suits were as integral to Yosemite Valley scenery as Half Dome, and his "tourist coach" was seasonally in demand with visitors who listened, fasci-

Astoundingly, the irrepressible James Hutchings succeeded Clark as Yosemite Guardian. (Hutchings/SS Collection)

George Fiske and Galen Clark met in the 1860's, and after 1879 were as close as brothers. (SS Collection)

Clark was allowed to lease his home, to which he had added a lean-to kitchen. (SS Collection)

nated, to his quiet but informative comments. He was becoming a living legend, and his grave digging was considered an amusing eccentricity. Friends loved to tell anecdotes about him. A favorite was of the time a visitor said, "After all your years in Yosemite, Mr. Clark, I am sure you are a reliable weather forecaster. Tell me, will it snow tomorrow, and is the winter going to be heavy?" The Guardian's answer was prompt and wry, "Ask the new man who just came in; he knows as much as I do."

In January, 1887, he described the winter for the *Mariposa Gazette:*

> We have had very pleasant weather between the storms . . . Ice at Mirror Lake is about four inches thick and men are at work cutting and putting it up for use at the hotels next summer. Our little community of winter residents here consists of ten adults, six men and four women. We have a tri-weekly mail which regularly brings us the news from the great outside busy world. We are anxiously looking forward for spring to open the way for business to again commence here in Yosemite.

In the long winter evenings, he read books, principally on natural sciences. Autographed copies of Wheeler's *U.S. Geological Survey* and Jean Bruce Washburn's *Yo Semite and Other Poems* were presented to him by their authors. Swedenborg's *Divine Love and Divine Wisdom*, published in 1883, was in his library too. Swedenborg's belief that natural objects were expressions of spiritual cause must have been in accordance with Clark's concept of "God in Nature." He felt that tangible miracles encircled him and that the "stern majesty of God's surrounding presence" influenced all in the Valley. He wrote:

> worshippers may come from all the world, the believers in sacred truths taught in the Holy Bible, the Roman, the Vedas, and the Zend Avesta, and bow in unison in the worship of the eternal and universal Father, the Creator of all, who understands the language of the soul, and gives his blessings to all alike who obey his laws.

While Clark enjoyed semi-retirement, the administration of the Yosemite Grant was suffering from an overdose of politicians. Hutchings' "unalloyed happiness" at being back in Yosemite Valley was short, for both his elder daughter, only eighteen, and his second wife died in 1881, just months after his assumption of the guardianship. His tenure in that post was marked by improvements in carriage roads, and the State's purchase of toll trails and roads which were, thereafter, free to the public. Clark had been promoting that for years,

Today, the site of Clark's Valley home is marked by the depression from his cellar and the tall cedar that flanked it. (Dean Shenk)

but appropriations had not been voted, as they were, at last, during Hutchings' time. His personality, however, earned him new opposition from his fellow commissioners, and he was ousted in 1884 after only three years of service. Hutchings' singular devotion to, and promotion of, Yosemite was unquestioned, but he possessed little subtlety and was too dictatorial for his fellow Commissioners, who were political appointees, mostly lacking background in Yosemite affairs. In October, 1884, after some dispute with his successor, Hutchings moved back to San Francisco where he returned to the tourist business, kept a critical eye and voice on the management of the Grant, and began a comprehensive book on it. *In The Heart of the Sierras*, published in 1886, contained these kind words about Clark: "He will be found intelligent, obliging, and efficient in everything he undertakes."

Hutchings' replacement was a transportation company official, Walter S. Dennison, who lasted only two years. Among the unpopular things he did was to allow over-grazing and ploughing so that the meadows were mere stubble. Also he removed the extensive piping in the Cosmopolitan bathhouse and saloon, which he turned into a combined residence and office. In 1887, Dennison was succeeded by Mark L. McCord, who had no particular qualifications for the position, but was an employee of the all-powerful Southern Pacific Company.

Both men were political appointees with no prior experience or knowledge of Yosemite; their regimes were studded with poor public relations, ill-advised regulations, and a "caretaking" that led to great criticism. During these two Guardians' years in office, the Legislature voted $40,000 to build the large, ornate three-story Stoneman House, named for the governor, to replace Black's and Leidig's run-down hotels, which were dismantled in 1888. After that the supposedly first class Stoneman and Barnard's Hotel, formerly Hutchings', were the only hotels in the Valley, which meant tourists had to pay $4.00 per day or camp out because no second-class place existed. Landscape artist Charles Dorman Robinson, who spent summers painting in Yosemite, was a self-styled crank as well as an ally of Hutchings'. Outraged by what he termed destruction, he led a campaign against the Yosemite Commissioners. His violent newspaper charges, accompanied by photographs, culminated in a February, 1889, investigation by the California Senate. Robinson advanced twenty-two charges of mismanagement, such as cutting and destroying timber for personal gain, disfiguring natural features, and fencing of farm land. They were answered by more than thirty witnesses in 430 published pages. In his lengthy testimony, Galen blamed neither of his successors. He emphasized that the State should administer

Clark prepared his own gravesite next to the monument for his friend Jim Lamon. (SS Collection)

At seventy-five, Clark was re-elected Guardian of the Yosemite Grant. (Carleton Watkins, YNP Collection)

the Yosemite Grant so that it

> should not be managed for the purpose of making money, because it is a section of California that California should be proud of . . . There is no place in the United States that draws so many tourists; there is no State which commands the admiration throughout the world . . . as . . . Yosemite Valley and its grand surroundings; and the State should take so much pride in its management as to be willing to appropriate liberally toward all the improvements necessary there, and charge but very little rental for any kind of business there.

Rightfully, he defended his own tenure, explaining that constant lack of State funds had hampered progressive administration. He criticized the system that had allowed ten-year leases to litigants like Hutchings, and yet granted other operators only yearly leases "which cramped them very much in their way of doing business."

Eventually Robinson's charges were dismissed as inconclusive and indefensible, but their furor removed the position of Guardian from politics. In a surprise move late on the night of June 6, 1889, McCord was fired and the Commissioners, including the governor, deliberated on a new guardian. They needed a man with integrity and no political connections or ambitions, a man with thorough knowledge of the grant and its concessionaires, a man who could be diplomatic yet forceful and impartial, someone with intelligence, wisdom, and compassion. That paragon existed in the person of Galen Clark, and he was selected by a vote of six to one. The *Gazette* summed up public approval:

> A more fitting appointment would be impossible. Mr. Clark . . . is familiar wih every inch of land, and every tree in and for miles around the Valley, and is well-acquainted with all the lessees. He knows how the visitors should be treated and withal is an educated, refined, moral and upright gentleman. He is a great lover of nature and will not permit natural beauties to be ruthlessly destroyed in order that some person may derive a pecuniary profit . . .

At seventy-five, Galen re-entered public life in his former job as Guardian of what he thought of as miracles of God and Nature — Yosemite Valley and the Mariposa Grove of Big Trees.

CHAPTER X

Guardian Again

▪

Back in official harness, Clark lost no time in instituting some of the changes he had long advocated. Within two months of his election, he had a crew of men cutting trees overhanging Mirror Lake and dredging out a sand bar that cut the lake in two. With the Commissioners behind him and appropriations to make improvements possible, he saw to it that a new road was built alongside the lake, repairs made on the Stoneman House, which had been poorly constructed, and clearing done in the Mariposa Grove. A year later, he supervised the erection of guard rails on the brinks of cliffs, an installation he had urged for years so timid people could appreciate views without fear. He took pleasure in the accomplishments, and the relieved Yosemite Commissioners so appreciated his dedication that the following June they reelected him unanimously and applauded him officially:

> The Executive Committee expressed its very cordial approval of the intelligence, industry and disinterested devotion displayed by Guardian Galen Clark.

Although his hearing had begun to fail and he had to wear reading glasses, his physical prowess, horsemanship, and lack of fear amazed people. He would stand on the edges of cliffs, guide tourists up steep trails, and reportedly, "until the last few years of his life he could shin up a tree as easily as a boy of 10." Not even heavy

snow immobilized him as he snowshoed throughout the Valley on oval Canadian or circular Indian-type snowshoes.

However, he was weary of Yosemite winters on the cliff-shaded southside of the Valley. As early as February, 1879, he had written for the *California Farmer:*

> I do not wonder that the old Persian Pharisees and astrologers were sun worshippers. I am very near being one myself, after living so long within the frigid shadows of these cold, towering granite rocks, mostly sheeted with ice and snow, and corrugated with frozen cascades. It is all very grand for a while, but it soon makes one feel chilly, and his soul yearns for the bright and warm sunshine.

When he heard that his friend Zachary Croop had moved to a new settlement in Santa Barbara County, he wrote requesting information. Croop had been a Merced neighbor of the Lees, and a carpenter for the Washburns at Wawona. His reply was enthusiastic. Summerland was on the hills beside the Pacific Ocean, six miles below Santa Barbara, and had a balmy winter climate. It was an infant beach town with less than twenty homes on its 1,000 hilly acres. It had been established by promoter H.L. Williams in 1886 as a haven for Spiritualists. That, as well as warm weather, attracted Clark, as he had been interested in the occult for years.

Clark's Point, named for the Guardian, is off this trail to Nevada Fall. (YNP Collection)

Clark's winter home was among the first in Summerland, where Spiritualism and oil proliferated. (Regan Family Collection)

His reading, and marriage to a fortune teller had deepened his knowledge. Charlie Leidig, son of the hotel-keeping Leidigs, claimed "that for a time Galen and some others in Yosemite were attracted to Spiritism," and Croop's daugther, May Lambert, stated firmly that Galen was a member of the cult. Daniel Foley confirmed this in writing: "Mr. Clark's religion was a high order of Spiritualism, and on his table of late years lay New Thought literature, but of it he seldom spoke."

Galen journeyed to Summerland, selected a hillside home site, and on July 8, 1890, paid Williams $160 for the four adjoining 50- by 100-foot lots. Then, according to the town's paper, he told Croop "what kind of house he wanted, waited until the plan was drawn, and never came back until the house was finished." A month earlier natural gas and petroleum springs had been discovered in Summerland, and soon its cultural intent was lost in the production of "black gold." In subsequent years, Clark's old speculative interest was roused and he invested money in more town lots, sure that oil would bubble up on one of them. As usual, his optimism was confounded by ill luck; weeds, not oil, came up on his property.

Despite that disappointment, Clark was solvent and debtless, possibly for the first time in his life. He was saving enough from his $125-per-month salary to finance the lots and construction of a home. Although Croop finished the house before winter, Clark did not go to Summerland, but spent the winter of 1890-91 in Yosemite. It is probable that he stayed because abruptly the Commissioners' responsibility was for a park *within* a park, and that involved the Guardian.

Aside from the year 1864, when the Yosemite Grant was established, 1890 was the most momentous time in the history of the region, as on October 1, 1890, Congress created Yosemite National Park. This National Park was composed of nearly a million acres of invaluable forests and watershed surrounding the original Grant.

This monumental act was a direct result of Muir's visit to Yosemite in June, 1889, with *Century Magazine* editor Robert Underwood Johnson. Both men were outraged at what sheep had done to the high country, and man, with fences, hayfields, and the pretentious, shoddy Stoneman Hotel, had done to the Valley. Both voiced their indignation and concern in *Century* and other influential periodicals, and thus spearheaded a quick and successful campaign for a national park. Clark, Hutchings, and the 1880 Yosemite Commissioners had stirred interest and introduced bills toward the same end. Even C.D. Robinson's exaggerated 1889 charges had dramatized the need for protection.

Although Clark had guard rails installed to protect people on Glacier Point, he ventured out on the overhanging rock, even in snow and ice. (YNP Collection)

This picture of Clark's Summerland home was taken in 1981, ninety-one years after the house was built. (Paul Diederich)

Thereafter, Galen was Guardian of the State Grant within a Federal Park as units of Army cavalry, with headquarters near Wawona, supervised the vast, new acreage in summers and two forest rangers, forerunners of today's park rangers, were custodians the rest of the year. This dual control added problems as fires, sheep, cattle, and hunters were no respecters of boundaries.

Clark's worth was recognized again in 1891 by the Commissioners. Not only did they reelect him unanimously, but also named a promontory overlooking Vernal Fall in his honor. As he had rerouted the trail to Nevada Fall so visitors could appreciate this vantage point, it was appropriate that Point Clark, later Clark's Point, perpetuated him.

In 1892, John Muir inspired the organization of the Sierra Club and became its first president. Its primary purpose was "To explore, enjoy, and preserve the Sierra Nevada and other scenic resources of the United States and its forests, waters, wildlife, and wilderness . . ." Although Galen was not a charter member, he belonged to the club for many years, and according to the Sierra Club *Bulletin* for 1904, he had charge of the Club's headquarters in 1893. If so, his care-taking must have been cursory indeed as his own responsibilities kept him fully occupied.

Paperwork — itemization of expenses, monthly reports and the like — kept him bending over his desk, writing in his straightforward legible hand in between interruptions and inspection trips. "During Galen Clark's second term as guardian . . ." Yosemite resident Laurence Degnan reminisced, "his office, in the large, bright, cheery front room of the departed saloon, with its glass doors, became a sort of club or lounging room,

well patronized by the men of the village and by visitors. Clark had a large table there, covered with newspapers and magazines, while a huge stove in the middle of the room was a popular attraction on cold winter evenings."

Another attraction was the massive Grand Register, a foot thick, introduced when John Smith operated the Cosmopolitan, in which visitors entered their names by the State they lived in. Its famous signatures and varied comments make interesting reading, although today, archives-bound, it is far less accessible.

In his lengthy annual reports to the Yosemite Valley Commissioners, Clark tried to explain the unfavorable criticism so often directed at them. Sometimes, as in the closing paragraph of his 1892 report, there was little defense:

> But so far as they [published criticisms] refer to the destruction of everything destructable (sic), by loose stock, as expressed by John Muir, they are not wholly false. The Yosemite Commissioners have adopted and published some most excellent By-laws, Rules, and Regulations for the Government and preservation of the Yosemite Valley, and Mariposa Big Tree Grove. Rule 18 specifies that no horses, cattle, or stock of any kind, shall be allowed to run at large within the Grant except under permission given in writing to the owner or owners thereof,
>
> But as there is no penalty affixed for its violation every successive Guardian has been powerless to enforce it, and ever will be until some other suitable coersive measures are brought to bear upon the owners of stock in Yosemite.

Daniel Foley began publication of the weekly *Yosemite Tourist* in 1891 when he established the Yosemite Falls Studio near the Guardian's office. Not only did Foley take pictures and sell them, but he had a little print shop in his studio. There he printed his paper and the yearly *Yosemite Souvenir & Guide*, which he wrote and edited with lively style. Clark's exploits, such as his April, 1891, "jaunt" of nineteen miles through snow to see if the new horse trail to Clouds Rest was passable, were included. As the years progressed, Galen told Foley stories of his past and even wrote an account of his discovery of the Mariposa Grove that appeared in Foley's guidebook for years.

Elvira's husband, George P. Lee, died in July, 1891, and despite heat, seventy carriage loads of friends and the Merced City Band turned out for his funeral and burial. In December, *The Summerland*, a Spiritualist newspaper, recorded that Clark and Mrs. Lee had arrived in town by train. "Mr. Clark has had a residence here for a year or more . . . which he had never seen until his arrival . . ." From the station, he could see his two-story, peaked-roof house looming alone on the bare hillside. A covered porch encircled three sides of the redwood structure, making it look larger than it was. A wide but steep staircase, opposite the front door, led to three bedrooms, and downstairs consisted of a living room, dining room, and kitchen. All six rooms had high ceilings, and double-hung windows facing superb views of the ocean, the Channel Islands, and the coastline. A well, wood stoves, lanterns, and an outhouse constituted conveniences.

Although the place was palatial compared to his Yosemite cabin, Galen was not satisfied, and the December 31 *Summerland* noted, "Mr. Galen Clark has ordered a basement and cistern constructed under his new house. Operations to remove the ground were begun at the beginning of last week." How long Elvira

lections, and learn about nature. Galen enjoyed his informal teaching, and the children delighted in it and him.

Perhaps those encounters helped Galen to decide on traveling east to visit his own grandchildren — the sons and daughters of his daughter Mary Ann Clark Regan and her husband, John. In June, 1893, the Yosemite Commissioners granted him a two-month leave with pay. In July, he left for a tour of Yellowstone National Park, a visit to the World's Columbian Exposition in Chicago, of which his old friend Olmsted was landscape architect, visits with the Regans in Connecticut and various Clark relatives in New Hampshire and

By 1895, Upper Village, with stores, offices, a stone jail, and the Sentinel Hotel complex, was the hub of Yosemite Valley activity. (George Fiske, SS Collection)

remained in residence is not known, but Clark stayed until spring.

When Croop had asked "Why in the world would a man your age want a two-story house?" the mountaineer had told him he "'liked lots of room and was going to bring much of the Valley with him,' which he came near doing." There wasn't a mountain or pine tree outside, but inside he had sequoia cones, sugarpine cones, slabs of bark, chunks of moss, arrowheads, rock specimens, and pressed wildflowers. May Croop Lambert recalled that each winter Clark brought more natural artifacts from Yosemite until all rooms and the basement were full. In addition the walls were adorned with choice landscapes of Yosemite. After school, the Summerland children swarmed to his porch or the summerhouse for stories of Yosemite, Indians, and mining, to see his col-

Massachusetts.

As he aged, some old-timers considered him colorless and mild-mannered, but that he was neither was obvious. Early in 1894 a *San Francisco Examiner* article by Hutchings aroused his wrath. A portion of the complaint ran:

> We have recently returned from the Yo Semite Valley, my wife and I, and we are both filled with regret and indignation at the so-called "management" there. Vandalism the most pronounced, with neglect that is positively criminal, and an indifference to results that is appalling . . . I am grieved to say are unrestrainedly rampant in the marvelous Valley.

> Thus, one by one these priceless gems [trees]

71

are being ruthlessly plucked from Yo Semite's unequalled diadem. When? O! When? will the Deliverer come? When will an indignant public rise to the situation, and, in the interests of the great State who has such a wonder within its boundary, wrest the whole and profitable heritage from the hands of its destroyers?

The rest of the melodramatic piece was replete with cases of individual trees that had been "sacrilegiously" cut, and reiterated phrases like "Alas, Alas," and "When? O! When? will the Deliverer come?"

Ever since 1866, Hutchings had tried Galen's patience and complicated his duties, but to criticize his guardianship, charging vandalism, was unendurable to a man who had loved and served Yosemite as long and wholeheartedly as had Clark. On February 18, 1894, he exploded to the *Examiner:*

> I would respectfully ask the favor of a small space in your valuable paper to make . . . some explanation and also corrections of some of the statements made by Mr. J. M. Hutchings in his article relative to vandalism in Yosemite published in the Sunday Examiner of the 11th inst . . . I wish to state that the oak trees referred to by Mr. Hutchings as having been cut for firewood last season, were cut solely by my permission. The Yosemite Commissioners had no knowledge of it whatever until after it was done.

Some of the trees were entirely dead from the blighting effects of misteltoe, and the others gave evidence of remaining life in a few small branches. In the exercise of discretionary judgement I considered it better for the future interests of Yosemite that these old decaying trees should be cut down and utilized as firewood so as to give the young growth of surrounding oaks a better chance to grow and develop more symmetrically. . . if the cutting of these old decaying trees can justly be construed as an act of vandalism or desecration of Yosemite's scenic beauty I wish all the blame and censure to fall upon myself alone. When Mr. Hutchings makes the statements that large patches of fragrant azaleas, Ceanothus and Syringas . . . have been exterminated 'as brush' for the sole purpose of adding increased facilities for pasture he certainly makes a great mistake, for no work has been done at clearing and exterminating 'brush' of any kind in Yosemite during the past year. And at no previous time has any of the flowering shrubbery in Yosemite been cut to my knowledge. On the contrary every possible precaution has been taken, under strict orders from the Yosemite Commission, to protect and preserve it from destruction or harm. With regard to the rebuilding of the Bridge across the Illilouette Creek at the top of the Falls — when Mr. Hutchings was in Yosemite in August last, the

The Sentinel Hotel complex was a bustling place in the late 1800's. (YNP Collection)

timbers for the bridge were all out ready to be put in place, and a few days later a good substantial Bridge was completed . . . Nature's wonderful prolific power in reproducing and enlarging the area of young forest growth in Yosemite is most marvelous, and if left entirely unchecked, the valley in a few years, comparatively, would become a veiled tangled wilderness. If Yosemite is to be maintained as a Park for public resort and recreation, a careful and judicious use of the axe and fire will be absolutely necessary.

While Mr. Hutchings was living in Yosemite keeping a Public House and running his sawmill, he had more trees cut than has ever been cut since by all the other residents who have lived in the Valley. He had to have milk cows to supply his table with milk and butter. Their increase soon amounted to a great herd. With energetic enterprise he organized a train of saddle animals for the special accommodation of his own guests. His cattle and horses roamed at large every season while he lived here, 'feeding at pleasure in the great pleasure ground of the Public, exterminating the rare grasses and unique Flora that once so delighted the vision of visitors.' [Hutchings] continued to work against the interests of Yosemite until a change in the commissioners took place and he got the appointment as Guardian. These frequent outbursts of morbid sentimentalism relative to the management of Yosemite, which find expression in the Public News Papers, are false in facts, malicious in character, and inspired by a very sentiment rather than a refined love of Nature and Yosemite.

Respectfully,
Galen Clark

Hutchings, ever resilient, was writing a guidebook, which was published in 1894. From 1890 on, at each of the Commissioners' annual June meetings, Hutchings applied for a lease on his old, unused cabin. Each year permission was deined "for reasons," the 1890 minutes read, "that will be obvious to any member of the Commission who will consult the records . . ." and because "no portion of the Valley is to be devoted to merely personal residence."

After five such denials, Hutchings pleaded his case to both branches of the State Legislature who gave him permission to occupy the cabin for one year or more beginning in 1895. Due to the determined, almost vitriolic opposition of Commissioner John P. Irish, and the fact the Board would not grant the $200 Hutchings requested to put the place in order, he was obstructed, and the lease was cancelled in 1897.

Inevitably, progress reached Yosemite Valley. After 1896 a railroad terminal was as close as Raymond, only

Few persons mourned the 1896 burning of the poorly planned and shoddily built Stoneman House. (SS Collection)

fifty-five miles away. Telegraph lines had been installed in 1875, and telephones followed in 1891. Electricity did not arrive until 1902 when a power plant was built at Happy Isles. The Upper Village-had progressed into a bustling place with a general store, photography studios, the Sentinel Hotel complex, a dynamite storage house that doubled as a jail, a blacksmith shop, workshops, the State barn, and the Degnan home and bakery. All these buildings and their sanitary systems, if any, were under Clark's jurisdiction.

One time he appeared at the Degnan home with a black eye, bruised forehead and nose. Of course he was questioned as to cause, and told young Laurence that "while he was groping for a door one pitch black night, with both arms outstretched, the door. . . smacked him . . . right in the face. Clark, with his pleasant, whimsical sense of humor, added that he was astonished to discover that his nose was longer than his arms!"

Private campers were increasing, and Clark wrote, "A small percentage of them commit acts of malicious mischief and even serious damage . . ." So troubling was this that in 1895 he asked the Commissioners for assistance. "One or two of the mounted patrol men now in Yosemite during the season of the most visitors would have a great restraining influence on this lawless class . . ."

The proliferation of services and residents, plus over 3,000 visitors a year, added so many winter responsibilities that Clark had to forego the 1895 winter in Summerland. He was eighty-two in March, 1896, and contemplated retirement, but first he wrote recommendations for the care of the Grant:

. . . Outside and independent of the regular heavy annual expenses of keeping the carriage-

These stalwart ice cutters were a cross-section of the Yosemite community. From left, Charlie Atkinson, unknown man, Jack Leidig, John Degnan, Sr., stagedriver Joe Ridgeway, and Roland Dexter stand in front. Tom Gordon is third from left in the back row, and John Degnan, Jr., is fourth. (Bonney P. Douthit Collection)

roads, trails, bridges, and buildings in safe repair, the old wooden stairway at the Vernal Falls which is now unsafe for use, will have to be replaced by a new set, either iron or wood. Some efficient system for the protection and preservation of the banks of the Merced River . . . from the strong flood currents in the early part of the season is most imperatively required.

All the open meadow ground . . . is being covered with young cottonwoods and willows and the drier portions of the Valley overrun with dense thickets of young pines and cedars. The great work of reclamation should be commenced as soon as possible, and prosecuted from year to year, until the whole Valley is again restored to its original superior beauty . . .

Unlike Hutchings and C.D. Robinson, who believed in sparing the axe to protect Yosemite, Galen repeatedly urged its use. Elsewhere, he had written that the

constant, vigilant care for the preservation of Yosemite has resulted in the whole valley being overrun with a young growth of trees and bushes, which, if not checked in their luxuriant, wanton growth, will certainly be a great damage to the best general interests of Yosemite as a public park.

On August 24, 1896 the ill-conceived, ill-starred Stoneman House burned to the ground, which signaled

more investigations and reports for Clark. Furthermore that loss meant overcrowding of the Sentinel Hotel's four buildings. Plumbing in them was inadequate, and he had problems with the manager on repairs and maintenance. Hassles were not compatible with either Clark's temperament or his age.

Although he had objected in the previous June, the Commissioners had once more unanimously reelected him Guardian. He felt honorbound to complete the year, but on October 19, 1896, he wrote Governor James H. Budd, ex-officio member of the Yosemite Commissioners:

I desire to give you and the Yosemite Commission timely notice that I do not wish to be considered a candidate for reappointment to the honorable position of Guardian of Yosemite Valley and Mariposa Big Tree Grove at your next annual June meeting in Yosemite. I fully realize that my physical condition is such that I cannot in all respects perform all of what I consider my duties successfully to my own entire satisfaction. I feel such a deep interest in Yosemite and its management that I wish at the close of this term to retire in favor of a younger and I trust more effective man whom you may in the meantime select for appointment.

Yours with cordial esteem and respect,

Galen Clark
Guardian
Yosemite, Calif.

CHAPTER XI

Mr. Yosemite

.

Clark delayed his departure for Summerland until after the November election so he could vote, as usual, Republican, and also as usual, serve as inspector on the board. Whether acting as inspector, notary public, official issuer of burial permits, justice of the peace, or clerk of the school board, his duties were fulfilled faithfully and meticulously before and after his retirement as guardian. Once the twenty-two Yosemite votes were properly recorded, he set off for the coast.

By then, Summerland boasted 700 residents attracted there by the oil as well as the climate. Derricks were things of beauty to speculators, but Clark's lots remained barren. Tank cars of oil were carried away by the Southern Pacific Railroad, and a fine wharf accommodated coastal steamers. Culture and education were not neglected; a church, grammar school, newspaper, library, and three lecture halls saw to that. The Spiritualists held many lectures, classes, and seances in the halls. Presumably Clark attended such meetings. Swedenborgianism was of equal interest to him, and he read and owned books on the doctrine of Scriptural revelations.

His house was surrounded by trees and shrubs he had planted, and he spent hours outdoors enjoying the balmy weather that contrasted so sharply with Yosemite temperatures. Whenever he went downtown, he donned a vest and suit coat. He took long walks along the beach, and was a regular patron of the town library.

"He was an inveterate reader," his friend May Lambert said, "and used to sit in his summerhouse and read by the hour, also in a rocking chair on his porch." Sometimes he took a train to Santa Barbara or Los Angeles. Once, while in Los Angeles, he called upon Jessie Benton Fremont and her daughter, and reminded them of their visit to Clark's Station in 1859, adding "that that musical night was among his most treasured memories . . ." A trained soprano, traveling with the Fremonts, had entertained them with operatic airs around a blazing camp fire.

No matter how content, comfortable, or warm he was in Summerland, when March breezes blew, Clark grew homesick, packed his satchel, and hurried back to Yosemite, even though March, and sometimes April, often featured snow.

His welcome home began at the railroad station in Raymond, terminus of a special Southern Pacific line serving Yosemite. The town, founded by the railroad and a hub of Henry Washburn's Yosemite Stage and Turnpike Company, was populated by hotelkeepers, stage drivers, and stablemen, most of whom knew and admired Clark. En route to Yosemite Valley, the stages made a lunch stop at his former headquarters, now the Wawona Hotel. There the Washburn brothers, and many of their employees, gave him a red carpet welcome. Clark's reactions to the change and success of the enterprise he had founded, struggled for, and lost were

Under the ownership of the Washburn brothers, Clark's Station evolved into the charming and successful Wawona Hotel, now more than a century old. (A. C. Vroman, Hank Johnston Collection)

masked by his customary courtesy and reserve. He was too wise a man to indulge in useless reflections, and the deference shown him was mindful of the present, not the failures of the past.

Back aboard stage, beside the driver if he wished, he was piloted over the familiar, long-planned road through mud and snow until arrival on the Valley floor. After that, massed pines, budding oaks and maples, and the frothing, spring torrent of river and waterfall fairly shouted welcome. At last, the junction of the Four-Mile Trail, George Fiske's house on the left, the Chapel on the right, and then a special stop in front of his home.

Because Fiske and (after 1897) his second wife Caroline took care of it while he was away, Clark found the inside free of cobwebs and mice. Soon heat from the stove banished dampness, and the sight and sound of Yosemite Falls was a final benediction to homecoming.

On June 3, 1897, Galen submitted his final Guardian's report. As had other reports, it stressed the necessity of clearing undergrowth, and revealed his steady accomplishments. Earlier he had summed up his philosophy as a public servant in these words: "I have endeavoured at all times to work in every way for the best inter-

ests of Yosemite, and accomplished as much as possible with the least amount of expense." His fellow Commissioners appreciated his words and deeds and, before the three-day meeting was over, presented him with a set of handsomely-inscribed resolutions commending his public service and wishing him "continued long life and constant happiness" in retirement. Part of it read:

> Whereas, his faithful and eminent services as Guardian, his constant efforts to preserve, protect and enhance the beauties of Yosemite; his dignified, kindly and courteous demeanor to all who have come to see and enjoy its wonders, and his upright and noble life, deserve from us a fitting recognition and memorial; . . . Therefore, be it resolved . . . That we recognize in him a faithful, efficient and worthy citizen and officer of this Commission and of the State . . .

The proclamation was widely published, but the State Legislature added neither approving words nor a deserved annuity for its officer. However, the Commissioners granted him a dollar-a-year lease on his cabin, as well as permission to use his carriage for hire.

Just prior to leaving Summerland, he had paid $400 for four more lots near the main road, which gave him a total of twenty. He had given up on oil, but knew he needed retirement income so had Croop build him two sturdy rental units facing El Camino Real. His planning was wise, but the construction was costly, and rental income low.

His Yosemite days contained a routine of purposeful activities: woodchopping, berry picking, cone collecting, some guiding, and lots of entertaining. Visitors stopped to talk, ask questions, take his picture, and obtain an autograph. "No sojourner in Yosemite Valley counted his visit complete," an admiring newspaperman wrote, "until he had shaken hands and chatted with Galen Clark . . . In this gray-bearded, kindly old man, there lived a wonderful soul." Many people left carrying a walking stick from a supply "he had cut and stripped. . ."

Clark was becoming an institution; a reliable, genial information bureau — Mr. Yosemite — whose charm lay in his modesty, dignity, and independence. Although he willingly posed for pictures, he told friends he couldn't understand why he should be an object of admiration.

At least once a week he spent several hours pumping and carrying water to the sequoias and flowers he had planted around his gravesite. A large, irregularly shaped boulder, on which his name was already chiseled, stood outside the stoutly fenced plot, an object of curiosity to children and adults. So great was Clark's regard for the Indians and their customs, and so obsessed was he with the intent of being properly buried, that he often told Fiske he wanted to be cremated amid brush and logs in the old Indian way, then have his ashes deposited in the grave.

His concern for the administration of the Yosemite Grant heightened as he observed the ineptness of the guardians who succeeded him. Miles Wallace lasted only two years. The *Mariposa Gazette* hoped that his replacement would not be another "useless fixture," but the next guardian, former stagedriver John Stevens, did what the Washburns, his former employers, wanted, which was not necessarily for the good of the Grant. While in office, Clark had opposed Army jurisdiction, writing:

> There are a few persons, who seem to be chronic faultfinders, that strongly advocate the policy of having Yosemite go back again to the United States Government, under the control of the Secretary of the Interior, but from what I have seen of the management of the Yellowstone Park, I think this would be a great mistake for the interest of Yosemite and the visiting public . . . I am sure that Yosemite can and will be much better managed for the public welfare by the State of California than by the United States Government.

In addition, he suggested that a master plan, by landscape engineers and photographic artists, be devised for Valley reclamation, and that the Board of Commissioners be limited to three men, "who should be appointed solely with reference to their special ability for the business, and who should receive a reasonable compensation for their services . . ." He was strongly of the opinion that three men, rather than eight, "would be more efficient in the execution of their duties and give better satisfaction."

By 1899, Clark was completely disenchanted with the State's continuing miserliness and inefficient political control. When the California Press Association adopted resolutions in favor of receding Yosemite Valley and the Mariposa Grove to the Government for inclusion in Yosemite National Park, he wrote a Vacaville newspaper expressing agreement. John Muir led the battle for recession, which was not won until 1905.

Occasionally one of the McCoys visited him, and in 1903, William Clark's daughter and Melzar Clark's son arrived from New Hampshire. Clark did everything he could to make their stay a memorable one. He took them to meet his Indian friends and to sample their acorn cakes. Sometimes Indians picked strawberries for him from patches originally planted by Hutchings. His daughter Elvira rarely visited, for she had moved to San Francisco, taken courses, and advertised herself as Dr. Lee, a metaphysician and cancer specialist.

Despite frugality, Clark found it hard to subsist on his meager income from rents in Summerland and collecting and selling seeds from pine cones in Yosemite. In the summer of 1900, therefore, he was custodian of the Sierra Club room at $35.00 a month. By 1901 his savings were almost gone, his horse and carriage* sold, and he was being forced to sell Indian baskets from his fine collection. His pride and poverty were noted by Henry Washburn and his business associate and brother-in-law, Jay B. Cook. Camp Curry, established in 1899, had proven such a success that they set up a similar camp amid a grove of oaks near the base of Yosemite Falls, and asked the 87-year-old man to be its manager.

When Camp Yosemite opened on May 15, 1901, Clark was in charge, but before long, hostess Frances Hickey took over, and gratefully Clark assumed less demanding tasks. As "Mr. Yosemite," fount of knowledge, he answered endless questions, charmed guests, prepared morning and evening campfires at which he presided, sprinkled the dust, carried mail back and forth from the post office, and even picked up litter. In return, he had three good meals a day, a bed when he wished to stay overnight, and pay. Porters received $30.00 a month plus room and board; Galen's salary could hardly have been less than theirs. He was universally liked; as one waitress said, "He takes great interest in everything . . . always doing something for others

---

*Clark's pioneer tourist coach is now on display at the Pioneer History Center in Wawona.

Frances Hickey and the ex-Guardian at Camp Yosemite about 1905. (Bonney Douthit Collection)

and trying to make people comfortable." After returning home, some guests remembered him with letters and gifts, and Miss Hickey was solicitous of him. For instance, his meals were served in the employee dining room where he was waited on by the pantry girl.

Camp Yosemite's season was short, usually from May 15 to mid-August or earlier if Yosemite Falls and its resultant creek stopped running, for the creek served as sewer. Improvements and enlargements were made each year until the camp boasted electric lights, a wash house, a "nice ironing stove," a bath-house with four bathrooms, and a dining room that could seat 200. No alterations were made in the primitive sewage system, however.

Once the camp closed, Clark added to his income by charging for guiding. In September, 1903, for example, W.W. Foote, a lawyer and Yosemite Commissioner, was amazed to find Galen guiding a party, including two small children, down the Four-Mile Trail from Glacier Point.

Clark's old adversary, James Hutchings, was still in and out of Yosemite, still a shrill, but earnest voice in criticizing its management, and, at eighty-two was

managing the hotel in the Calaveras Grove of Big Trees. His book, *In the Heart of The Sierras*, first published in 1886, had become the bible of Yosemite history, and his guidebook was popular. On October 31, 1902, while driving his third wife down the Big Oak Flat Road in a buggy, his team shied and bolted. The old pioneer was thrown upon the rocks, where he managed to say, "I am very much hurt," before dying. He died as he had lived, dramatically, and was buried beside his daughter and second wife in the Pioneer Cemetery.

A happier event took place in Yosemite in May, 1903, when President Theodore Roosevelt roughed it on a camping trip with John Muir. Their talk and examination hurried recession as thereafter Roosevelt dealt forcefully with the issue.

Sometimes admirers wanted to give Clark money, but his independence and reserve were so obvious that they dared not offer. At least once, in the fall of 1903, his uncompromising integrity blocked recompense. After forester T.P. Lukens had written to request a certain kind of pine cone seeds, Clark hunted for them without success in both Hetch Hetchy Valley and the Mariposa Grove of Big Trees. Despite the considerable expenditure of time, travel, and energy, he wrote Lukens:

> I have received your check for ten dollars which I beg leave to return to you herewith. I have no charge against you for any little favor extended to you, and cannot take anything in advance for what I might fail to get.

This autonomy and aversion to borrowing, his horror of debt, were an outgrowth of the bad years when he had to borrow, even beg for loans, never fully repaid, from his brothers. After the mortgages and failure at the South Fork, his self-respect demanded self-sufficiency, but that unbending quality was hard on well-wishers who longed to make his life easier.

Commissioner Foote and businessman Charles Burnett concocted a plan to circumvent Clark's pride, utilize his knowledge, and aid him financially all at the same time. They promised to supply capital and attend to publishing details if he would write a book about Yosemite. Instead of narrating his own experiences, he wrote about his Indian friends, describing their customs and history. His text evolved into a handsome, pocket-sized, well-illustrated book, which was published just before his ninetieth birthday, March 28, 1904. He left Summerland in time to be guest of honor at a combined birthday-publication party at artist Chris Jorgenson's Yosemite Valley home. Jorgenson had made drawings depicting Indian life, his wife had designed the book cover, and Fiske, Foley, and Boysen had contributed photographs.

Paperback copies sold for 50 cents, hardbound for $1.00, and advance orders amounted to almost 1,000 copies. After Burnett had reported the sales, he presented Clark a check of over $400. Then his mother, Julia Burnett, read a five-stanza poem she had written in Clark's honor. One verse ran:

> And though he has already richly won
> More than his gentle soul would claim,
> At ninety has a new career begun
> That adds the title 'Author' to his name.

Soon after publication, the modest author wrote T.P. Lukens, "I am glad you like the little book. I was induced to write it somewhat against my will, well knowing that I am not a good Bookwriter." In this opinion, he was right. Unhappily, the most interesting portion of the text was the account of the author's life, which Foote had completed only days before he died. The significance of the book lay in its collection and retelling of beliefs and ceremonies known to Clark because of his friendship with the Ah-wah-nee'-chees. There were no personal experiences, no anecdotes or characterizations of individual Indians. The explanations were informative and factual, but phrased in a

Both Clark's handwriting and his message were clear. (From Dorothy Atkinson's autograph book, Courtesy Bonney B. Douthit)

"A little bit of Patience often makes the sunshine come,
a little bit of Love makes a very happy home,
a little bit of Hope makes a rainy day look gay,
and a little bit of Charity makes glad a weary way"
Sincerely your Friend
Galen Clark

Yosemite Sept 5th 1905

"Mr. Yosemite" in a moment of repose. (Hutchings/SS Collection)

simple, pedestrian way. It is sad that a ghost writer wasn't provided to elicit the fascinating past from its participant. In his earlier newspaper writings, Clark had been effusive, sometimes amusing, certainly interesting, and often positive and outspoken, but modesty, reticence, and age had limited his ability to write outstanding, revealing history.

Nevertheless, because of his popularity and the respect people had for him and his new endeavor, the little book sold. Even though it was prosaic, its text was lucid, intelligent, and accurate — a remarkable feat for a man of such age. "Please do not let the sale of my book interfere with that of your own guide book," Clark told Foley, once again illustrating his self-effacing, unselfish spirit. Copies were sold in all the photography studios or could be purchased from the author himself. His income would have been far greater if he had not given away so many copies.

Burnett and others insisted that his career continue, after Camp Yosemite closed in mid-August of 1905, he journeyed by stage to examine the sequoia groves in Sequoia National Park. He wanted to investigate them before describing various groves in his second book, *The Big Trees of California*. Upon his return home, he wrote a friend that he had been away a month, and

> . . . enjoyed my trip very much . . . the trees are very numerous and in a fine state of preser-

vation, not being so badly injured by fires as in most of the groves north.

> I am glad that a few of these remaining giant trees, a connecting link between the present and a prehistoric Botanical age, are being preserved and protected from destruction by the lumber syndicates and trusts who love and worship golden Eagles *above all other hallowed gifts of nature.*

His vitality, energy, and zest were youthful, yet winters and germs were his downfall. While visiting Elvira in San Francisco in March, 1905, for example, newspapers reported him "lying dangerously ill." By summer, he had made an amazing recovery and was back working at Camp Yosemite. He slowed down a bit, for instead of spending several hours a week pumping and carrying water to the plantings around his gravesite, he hired a teenage boy to do the job. Elvira insisted that he spend the 1905-06 winter with her, and he agreed, which indicated his awareness of frailty. By early April, he was again prostrated by "la grippe," and the complications frightened Elvira, who used all her medical skills to treat him.

In the pre-dawn hours of April 18, she "was up and dressed and trying to relieve" her father's pain when a jolting earthquake shook the city. The house was undamaged, but they fled outside where Elvira made him a bed of blankets on the sidewalk until it seemed safe to return inside. Her version of events, as written to her sister, Mary Ann, was more dramatic than the laconic recital Clark later made to Foley, who, of course, printed it in his *Yosemite Tourist*. About 4 a.m. the 19th, soldiers ordered them to leave because the earthquake-caused fire was nearing. They carried as many belongings as possible, and started toward the Bay on foot. Elvira said "they were driven nearly all day and sometimes could not stop more than five minutes at a time." She feared her father "would surely succumb" from the stress and exhaustion. A few crackers and a little water were all they had to sustain them. Clark admitted that "he had to rest many times in going a block."

Finally, nearly twelve hours after they had left the house, they boarded a ferry for Oakland where they recuperated at the home of friends. Plates and negatives of Clark's Indian book were burned, and only 200 copies of the second edition saved. Despite the loss, fear, and danger, a rejuvenated Clark, back in Yosemite by early May, told Foley, "I would not have missed it for anything in the world."

The remainder of 1906 was far less traumatic. It was Clark's last summer at Camp Yosemite. Trudging back and forth for the camp's mail, and continually being with people was over-taxing. No matter where he went, people wanted to shake his hand and chat. Local children, white and Indian, loved him, and his pockets bulged with small trinkets or maple sugar for them.

Young Marjorie Cook liked to carry packages for him, but he always sent her home, she remembered, when they reached "the exact center of the meadow" between the village and his house. Spitfire Marjorie told him of a fistfight she had had with another girl, and he gave counsel. "My dear, your hate does not injure her. It is very damaging to you. Think of the energy you waste." Later, he wrote in her autograph book, "There is nothing so lovely as love and nothing so hateful as hate."

"I cannot see to write or read except in the best clear light," he told his sister. Thus, he wrote much of the manuscript for *The Big Trees of California*, which Burnett published for him in 1907, outdoors beside his cabin, although the location exposed him to the interruptions of by-passers. "He was always gracious and chatted with everybody," a niece said.

One of his favorite spots was a log on which he sat for long intervals, marveling at the ever-fascinating forms of the lower Yosemite Fall. Often the Sovulewski children, who lived nearby in the former Hutchings home, joined him. He told their father, Gabriel Sovulewski, that a bench should be placed there so tourists could relax as they marveled.

Some of his contemplations were of conservation. On the whole, he approved the Army jurisdiction of Yosemite National Park which had begun in 1906 after the recession of the Yosemite Grant. Neither civilians nor soldiers, in his opinion, were doing enough clearing to return the Valley to its enchanting, open shape. When he had first viewed it in 1855, he remembered,

> The Indians had kept the Valley clear of thickets of young trees and brushwood shrubbery so they could not be waylaid, ambushed or surprised by enemies from outside and to afford no hiding places for bear or other predatory animals, and also to clear the ground for gathering acorns . . .
>
> At the present time there is not more than one-fourth of the Valley clear, open ground . . .

In an article published in the April, 1907, *Sunset* Magazine, titled "Yosemite — Past and Present," he pled for judicious clearing, as well as "some thorough system of protection . . . to save the river banks from further damage." Later, part of his thoughtful treatise was repeated in his third book.

In the fall of 1907, Clark traveled to Oakland, instead of Summerland, so he could again enjoy the companionship and care of his daughter, who had opened a new office there. Her ads ran, "Dr. Elvira M. Lee, Electro-Therapeutist, Graduate of the College of Fine Forces, Also the World's Electro-Medical Institute, Home Treatment when desired." Her credentials were as shaky as the "colleges," which had taught "electric light baths" and "creative treatments." A correspondence course had instructed her about "electricity, heat, light, color, steam, ferromagnetism, and mind cures." Like her father, she was interested in Spiritualism and had pre-

Clark wrote these three little books when he was in his nineties. (Michael Dixon)

"The Yosemite Kids" was Fiske's title for this picture of him with his old friend Clark. (Mode Wineman, YNP Collection)

81

"Dr. Elvira Lee, Electro-Therapeutist," outlived her father by only two years. (Regan Family Collection)

monitions of disasters.

Soon after Christmas, 1907, at his daughter's home, Clark became ill, and remained sick for two months. Earlier, a medical doctor had told Elvira that her father "had a stronger hold on life than I had . . ." At a mere sixty-eight, she was often ill, quite deaf, overweight, and survived her father by only two years. Clark, as indomitable as ever, climbed out of bed, went across the Bay to witness the arrival of the U.S. Great White Fleet on May 7, 1908, and then hurried home to the healing air of Yosemite.

By then, he could ride a train all the way to a new railroad terminus in El Portal, seven miles below Yosemite Valley. Old friends of his, the William Sells, operated the Hotel Del Portal, a massive yet rustic structure situated above the railroad station, and repeatedly urged Clark to be their guest overnight. Once he surprised them by accepting, then spent half the next day ranging the hills to gather wildflower specimens for Mrs. Sell, in appreciation.

Will Sell, Jr., who in 1908 began operating Camp Ahwahnee, near the site of the former Leidig Hotel, was also daunted by the old man's independence. When Clark returned from Oakland in the spring of 1908, the stage stopped at the camp, and he was urged to stay for at least a meal. He refused, saying he must go open his house. There, a porter who carried Clark's bags for him, saw him munching on a piece of stale bread found in a cupboard.

One day, Sell was startled to see Clark at the camp's registration desk, asking to spend a night. Every care was shown him as a guest of honor, and Sell was determined not to accept payment. "I won't offer to pay," ever-independent Clark anticipated him the following day. "Friends had asked if this would be a good place to stay, so I came for firsthand information, and will now write them that indeed, Camp Ahwahnee offers splendid accommodations."

Only the ever-supportive McCoy nephews made inroads on his independence. His namesake, Galen Clark McCoy, frequently sent him small amounts of money which Clark kept and used. Age was diminishing his dignified appearance. He was balding, his beard was straggly, his eyes sunken in pouchy flesh, and his hearing and eyesight deteriorating. Nevertheless, he was working on his third book in the summer of 1909, but wrote his sister, "I could not see to write in the house and outside I was constantly interrupted by visitors." He added, "I am also getting to be of not much account generally."

However, in late August, he demonstrated the remarkable alertness and vigor of his ninety-five-year-old mind by giving a speech on the history of Yosemite to a State convention of County School Superintendents held in the Valley. Will Sell, Jr., was an impressed observer of Galen's ability to return to his main theme without hesitation or wandering despite the many interruptions of questions from the audience. Afterward, the *Mariposa Gazette* recorded, he was given an ovation, and the superintendents passed a resolution that his two books be placed on the State school list of supplemental readers.

During the winter of 1909-10 in Oakland, Galen finished his information-packed book, *The Yosemite Valley, Its History, Characteristics, Features and Theories Regarding its Origin.* His final chapter, "Hints to Yosemite Visitors," contained ideas such as,

> A soft felt hat is preferable to straw . . . A cloth traveling cap is the worst thing to wear. . . A week is the shortest time that should be allowed for a trip to the Yosemite . . . The grandeur of the Valley cannot be fully appreciated in a few days . . . Take a little more money than you think you will need. You may want to prolong your stay . . . Treat the Indians with courtesy and consideration if you expect similar treatment from them. Do not expect them to pose for you for nothing. They are asked to do it hundreds of times every summer and are entitled to pay for their trouble
> . . .

Early in March, 1910, Clark packed his manuscript and a number of Fiske's photographs into his suitcase, and boarded a train to Redondo Beach where Charles

*After their deaths, a memorial bench for Clark was placed near a plaque remembering his
friend John Muir. (SS Collection)*

Clark's old friend George Fiske, at right, shown here after the memorial service for the ex-Guardian at the Yosemite Chapel. (J. T. Boysen, Courtesy Bonney B. Douthit)

Burnett lived. After Foote's death, Burnett had cheerfully shouldered full responsibility for financing, publishing, and advertising Clark's books, and saw to it that the page design and border were beautifully done. Today's collectors prize the handsome, pocket-sized volumes.

On March 10, the *Los Angeles Times* reported on Clark's authorship, his significant life, and his plan to celebrate his ninety-sixth birthday at the Redondo Beach Hotel. While in Redondo Beach his inveterate curiosity and ever-zestful interest in progress led him on a tour of the new half-million-dollar heated bath house. There he became overheated, and Elvira later wrote that that had been the cause of catching a "terrible chill."

Galen labeled it a "very hard cold" to a distant relative, John Cutter, who visited him at the Natick House in Los Angeles. Despite his illness, he had made a trip to South Pasadena and told his caller he was going to Summerland soon. About then, a stage driver from Yosemite came in and, Cutter recorded, "I left them talking interestedly."

Instead of going to Summerland, Galen went directly to Oakland where Elvira could take care of him. On the afternoon of Thursday, March 24, four days before his birthday, he lay down to take a nap, thinking that his cold was better, that soon it would be April and time to return home. His token dollar bill, for lease of his cabin, had been sent to Major William W. Forsyth, Acting Superintendent of Yosemite National Park. As usual, George Fiske was seeing that neither rain nor rats damaged the place and that snow was cleared off its shingled roof. Galen remembered that there was rubbish to burn; a crackling bonfire, while the ground was still damp, would take care of that.

Yosemite Valley in April meant an uncertain spring with sudden snows and quick thaws, cry of the coyote and roar of the river, the ice cone breakup at the base of Upper Yosemite Falls, and what he had described as "the cheerful and pleasant aspect of spring" taking hold.

> The aeolian tones of the zephyrs playing
> through the foliage of the evergreens, the hum
> of the insect tribes . . . the warbled melody of
> the happy birds in the groves; the liquid notes
> of the crystal waves . . . the murmur of the
> gracious cascade . . . the deeper tones of the
> wind vibrating through the forests and moun-
> tain crags . . . the careless, varied roaring of
> the great waterfalls . . . to swell the grand
> 'anthem of welcome to nature's great festivals'
> . . .

All that and more was spring . . . he slept . . .

When Elvira entered his room at 6:00 p.m., she found her father asleep forever.

She summoned a doctor and an undertaker, notified her sister, Fiske, the McCoys, and Yosemite officials. Preparations were begun to send the body to the grave-

The sequoias he planted, and the children he loved, participated in last rites for Galen Clark. George Fiske stands behind children at left, James McCauley at right. (J. T. Boysen, Courtesy Bonney B. Douthit)

site so painstakingly prepared. A Dr. Fenton certified bronchial pneumonia as cause of death. Clark's lungs had finally failed him, fifty-four years after a doctor's prediction of imminent death.

Before Clark's body could be shipped, Major Forsyth had to request a burial permit from the Department of the Interior. In the interim, simple funeral services were held in the 11th Street house in Oakland.

Editorials and tributes praising Galen Clark's contributions as a private citizen and State official appeared in California's leading newspapers. Not a line was printed about his business failures, but many laudatory words described his public successes as a Yosemite pioneer, explorer, guardian, and conservationist. The *Los Angeles Times* claimed his death was a "notable event in the history of California," that his character had been "noble." The *San Francisco Chronicle* noted his prominence and his friendships with other important citizens. *The Mariposa Gazette* recited his many accomplishments and mourned his loss as the foremost Mariposa County personage, its oldest citizen and voter.

Daniel Foley wrote a telling tribute for the *Merced Evening Sun:*

> With the passing of Mr. Clark there is created a void in Yosemite and Big Tree affairs that cannot be filled . . . His knowledge of the general history of the people and conditions that made it, the flowers, birds, animals, trees and Indians cannot be duplicated by another living

person . . . I consider that Mr. Clark was the one man who really, truly loved Yosemite, not for what he could get out of it, but for itself, its wonder, its beauty . . . Like Yosemite, he was beyond words: too great to talk about, impossible to describe . . .

As soon as Elvira received word that a burial permit had been wired from Washington, she called the Oakland undertaker who escorted the coffin by railway to El Portal, then by stage to the Valley. On Saturday, April 2, Ernest P. Leavitt, Forsyth's assistant, gave the eulogy while Yosemite friends and their solemn white-garbed children looked on. After his talk, the children placed evergreen wreaths and cherry blossoms tied with purple ribbons on the casket. Then the pallbearers — Jay B. Cook, John Degnan, James McCauley, J.W. Coffman, J.T. Boysen, and Nelson Salter — added their boutonnieres. Slowly, the casket was lowered into the grave while nearby Yosemite Falls crashed down with its natural, wild organ peal of sound.

The finest memorial, quoted extensively in Chapter IV of this book, was written by John Muir for the June, 1910, *Sierra Club Bulletin.* In it he said that "Galen Clark was the best mountaineer I ever met," and "one of the most sincere tree-lovers I ever knew." At the end of the eloquent testimonial, he mentioned the sequoia seedlings that Clark had nurtured into "good, thrifty trees. Doubtless," he said, "They will long shade the grave of their blessed lover and friend."

85

As he planned, Clark rests in remembered peace, shaded by the sequóia trees he planted nearly a century ago. (Dean Shenk, 1981)

AFTERWORD

Galen Clark had not made a will, but several months before his death had deeded all of his Summerland property to his daughter Elvira who sold at least part of it just prior to her own death in November, 1912. Immediately after her father's death, she had asked the Fiskes to sell Clark's household effects "so that the money could be used for publishing his new book." C. H. Burnett wrote an introduction, and sketch of the author, for *The Yosemite Valley* and had it printed. Profits from it, and his previous books, went to Elvira and her sister Mary Ann Regan.

"Father expressed a desire to have most of the miscel-laneous items (books) remain in Yosemite," Elvira wrote the Army superintendent of Yosemite National Park, "as the possible nucleus of some future, large public library." For years his books, with the exception of the "new thought" ones which she took, were housed in LeConte Memorial Lodge, headquarters of the Sierra Club in Yosemite Valley. Finally, in 1979, the Club gave the bulk of Clark's collection to the Research Library of Yosemite National Park.

Even after ninety-six years, his worldly possessions were scanty in contrast to his contributions which were great.

Index

*Denotes Illustrations

Continued on page 88

Index Continued